# THE FRIENDSHIP OF
# A MOUNTAIN

PASCAL BRUCKNER

# The Friendship of a Mountain

*A Brief Treatise on Elevation*

Translated by Cory Stockwell

polity

Originally published in French as *Dans l'amitié d'une montagne. Petit traité d'élévation* © Éditions Grasset & Fasquelle, 2022

This English edition © Polity Press, 2023

Excerpt from Michel Tournier, *Célébrations* © Mercure de France, 1999. Included with permission of the publisher.

Excerpt from *L'Os à Moelle*, by Pierre Dac © Presses de la Cité, 2007, 2020 for the current edition. Included with permission of the publisher.

Excerpt from Sid Marty, 'Abbot', *Headwaters*, © McClelland and Stewart, Toronto 1973. Included with permission of the author.

Excerpt from *Mountains of the Mind: A History of a Fascination*, by Robert MacFarlane © Granta Books, 2003. Used with permission of the publisher.

Excerpt from *Mountains of the Mind: How Desolate and Forbidding Heights Were Transformed into Experiences of Indomitable Spirit*, copyright © 2003 by Robert Macfarlane. Used by permission of Pantheon Books, an imprint of the Knopf Doubleday Publishing Group, a division of Penguin Random House LLC. All rights reserved.

Polity Press
65 Bridge Street
Cambridge CB2 1UR, UK

Polity Press
111 River Street
Hoboken, NJ 07030, USA

ISBN-13: 978-1-5095-5553-6 – hardback

A catalogue record for this book is available from the British Library.

Library of Congress Control Number: 2022948504

Typeset in 11 on 13pt Sabon
by Fakenham Prepress Solutions, Fakenham, Norfolk NR21 8NL
Printed and bound in the UK by CPI Group (UK) Ltd, Croydon

The publisher has used its best endeavours to ensure that the URLs for external websites referred to in this book are correct and active at the time of going to press. However, the publisher has no responsibility for the websites and can make no guarantee that a site will remain live or that the content is or will remain appropriate.

Every effort has been made to trace all copyright holders, but if any have been overlooked the publisher will be pleased to include any necessary credits in any subsequent reprint or edition.

For further information on Polity, visit our website: politybooks.com

*To the memory of my friend Laurent Aublin (1949–2009), who introduced me to Asia and to climbing at high elevations. His benevolent spirit continues to accompany me on every path, at every summit.*

*For Anne, in memory of the ascent of the Aiguille du Tour.*

# Contents

# Acknowledgements

The expression *The Friendship of a Mountain* is taken from a novel by Jean Giono.

First and foremost, I'd like to thank Jean-Pierre Aublin and his brother Norbert, who hosted me for many years in Boucher, near L'Argentière in the Hautes-Alpes, for all the unforgettable moments.

I'd also like to thank Françoise and Hugues Dewavrin, whose gourmet hospitality in their chalet in Megève brightens our winters and our summers.

A huge and friendly nod to François Leray for his sense of pedagogy, his patience, and his true guide's loyalty.

A special nod to Frédéric Martinez in remembrance of the Écrins and the Pointe Percée.

A warm nod to Brieuc Olivier, the hermit of Bettex who every day clinks glasses with Mont Blanc.

A nod also to my faithful climbing companions Manuel Carcassonne, Serge Michel, and Pierre Flavian.

Finally – last but not least – a tender thought for my daughter Anna, who has been trudging about with her papa for so many years.

He who is not capable of admiration is contemptible. No friendship is possible with him, for there is only friendship in the sharing of common admiration. Our limits, our short-comings, and our small-mindedness are all healed when the sublime bursts forth before our eyes.

MICHEL TOURNIER

# Preamble: The Test of the Coconut Tree

Some time ago, I undertook, alongside a climbing companion, Serge Michel, the short ascent of Mount Thabor, which peaks at 3,171 metres. Thabor, which means pious in Aramaic, is also a site of pilgrimage on the French–Italian border, in the Hautes-Alpes. The chapel of Notre-Dame des Sept Douleurs, a solidly built if rather dilapidated building, stands at the summit, and embodies, for the believers, a distinctive site that is linked to the passion of the Christ. When you go there, you come across Buddhists in the lotus position, sitting right in the wind, seeking communion with the cosmos. Having left at about 11 o'clock from the Névache valley, we climbed across firns and screes, a task made all the more difficult by the August heat, which scorched us until we got above 2,500 metres. When we arrived at our destination late in the afternoon, and stood on the knoll at the summit that is covered in Tibetan flags, Serge said to me: 'You've done it. You've passed the test of the coconut tree.'

'The test of the coconut tree?'

'In certain tribes, the elderly are forced to take a test each year. They have to climb to the top of a coconut tree that the others shake vigorously. Whoever falls is driven out of the village, and goes off to die alone in the jungle.

Whoever makes it to the top is allowed to remain in the community.'

Ever since I heard these words, I've subjected myself to this test every year, so as to prove that I'm still in the game. There are two mountains I never stop climbing: an internal mountain that fluctuates, in my daily life, between joy and disarray, and an external mountain that confirms or belies the first one.

The descent of Mount Thabor was dangerous: lost on the wrong path, we came upon a herd of sheep, and were attacked by several aggressive sheepdogs. These dogs, which weigh between 90 and 100 kilograms, and which protect sheep and goats from wolves and bears, are extremely dangerous for walkers. It is recommended to avoid looking them in the eye so that the dogs, strong but touchy, don't think you're challenging them. Keep a low profile, don't brandish your walking sticks, look at the ground. We only escaped thanks to a mischievous groundhog who, from the other side of the river, whistled at the beasts, which scampered off after the rodent, determined to tear it to pieces. I recall now that the coconut tree, in Simenon's work, plays a different role. In a short book in which he sketches the lifestyle of colonizers who went overseas in the 1930s to escape the mediocrity of their home country, he mentions a peculiar use of this tropical tree: on certain Pacific islands, when a woman wants to show a man – above all a foreigner – that she consents to his advances, she climbs to the top of a coconut tree, exposing to her suitor everything he'll obtain – the sun and the moon – if he makes the effort to follow her up the tree.[1] It's a tradition that demands an effort, and we should reinstate it in our more temperate climates: it would encourage our municipalities to plant more trees in our stifling cities. It would at once prevent harassment and the laying of ever more concrete. Since that day, I've thought about the gracefully inclined coconut tree whenever I begin a climb, summoning this exotic tree to accompany me in the heart of the Alps or the Pyrenees.

Why climb when you're long past the summit of life, when you're already hurtling down the other side of the mountain? Why force yourself to undergo such ordeals, if not to take from them a joy verging on beatitude? It's not faith that raises mountains – it's mountains that elevate our faith in challenging us to overcome them. These hooded majesties crush some people while exalting others. For the latter, climbing means being born again, reaching a state of effervescence. Being seized by exhaustion upon arriving at the summit is akin to casting your eyes upon paradise. The density of the moment draws us in. Is it the stinging cold, the wind so strong that it smacks you and almost knocks you down – or is it higher powers that speak to us in this mixture of terror and beauty?

CHAPTER 1

# Where Goes the White When Melts the Snow?

The smallest snowstorm on record took place an hour ago in my back yard. It was approximately two flakes. I waited for more to fall, but that was it.

RICHARD BRAUTIGAN, *TOKYO MOUNTAIN EXPRESS*[1]

Do you hear the snow against the window-panes, Kitty? How nice and soft it sounds! Just as if some one was kissing the window all over outside. I wonder if the snow *loves* the trees and fields, that it kisses them so gently?

LEWIS CARROLL, *THROUGH THE LOOKING-GLASS, AND WHAT ALICE FOUND THERE*[2]

I was born into life in the continuous haze of flakes that summons forgetting and blissful sleep. Placed in a sanatorium at the age of two, a *Kinderheim* in the Vorarlberg region of Austria, because I was in the early stages of tuberculosis, I first came into contact with the world in the Alps, more specifically in the Kleinwalsertal, a high-altitude valley that, while officially part of Austria, is in fact an exclave located in Bavaria. Its summits rarely pass 2,500 metres – you have to go to Tyrol for the mountains that approach 4,000 metres. The cold, however, was intense: the winter temperatures of my childhood often plummeted to minus 20 or minus 25 for weeks on end. In the middle of January, the animals – stags, deer, chamois – would come down to lower elevations to visit houses where people would feed them hay. Seeing snow today brings me back to when I wore shorts, or rather *Lederhosen* (leather pants), and suspenders in the Bavarian style, and a strange little hat reminiscent of a kippa. Now that snow is growing rarer, I'm always very moved when this blessed powder honours us with its presence: I see in it the contours of my past. I spent my childhood in the centre of Europe for the worst possible reasons. My father, a passionate anti-Semite who adulated the Third Reich until his dying day in August 2012, wanted to make me a true Aryan. An engineer who chose to work for Siemens from 1941 until 1945, first in Berlin and then in Vienna, he fled the arrival of the Red Army, which arrived at the gates of the city in April 1945, and took refuge, along with his mistress, in the Vorarlberg, which was under French administration. He would send me there seven years later. Having escaped the pursuit of justice upon his return to Paris in November 1945 thanks to a bureaucratic error, he sought to avenge Germany's defeat by way of his offspring. My timely illness would allow me to settle his score. Unfortunately for him, I didn't fulfil his wishes. With my Teutonic family name, I was immediately Judaized in France and considered a Jewish intellectual, to his great despair. As someone who seemed to be resisting his own heritage – playing at being a goy – I entered, in spite of myself and in spite of my father, into the great Mosaic family that he would have liked to wipe out. No sooner did I protest that my background was Catholic than my borrowed identity was thrust back upon me. 'It's not a problem if you don't want to admit it!' I wonder if my father isn't laughing at this turn of events from beyond the grave.

Snow is inseparable from the pine tree, that zealous, unbending servant who barely moves, except when it relieves its branches by allowing its surplus of snow to fall. It's a discreet type of conifer: a green column loaded with thorns that keep us from approaching. It huddles together with its fellow pines, and when it bends in the assaults of the wind or a storm, it holds its boughs tight to its body, focused on its trunk like a greedy man on his treasure. Parsimonious and rustic, it groans as though it were inhabited by a crowd of ghosts who might at any moment arise from the undergrowth. This conifer truly appears to be a worker, carrying its parcels of snow like so many packages – a lackey of great height. It's a pencil covered in feathers, willing to be martyred every year to become a Christmas tree. We place candles on its branches, and we adorn it with tinsel, ornaments, roasted nuts, and flashing lights. We place piles of multi-coloured, useless gifts at its feet. It is destined to be sacrificed: we chop it down in the hundreds of thousands so it can play a bit part for a few days in apartments or houses. It smells nice at first, but ends up slumping on the sidewalk, before being cut up into pieces and taken to the dump. A massacre, all for the joy of children, whether young or old. A sped-up allegory of human existence. We've seen enough of you – now scram. This thrifty resinous tree, austere guardian of mountains, always appears apologetic, wondering what it's doing there. And as though it hadn't been sufficiently taken advantage of by humans, today some in France judge it to be too phallic, and want to replace the pine tree – *sapin* in French, a masculine word – by what they

3

call the *sapine*, an accessory of 'Mother Christmas' that is laid down horizontally rather than erected vertically. The French word, however, lends itself to inappropriate jokes, and highlights what it had sought to obfuscate.[3]

As soon as I get above 1,000 metres, I breathe better, and I feel a very particular euphoria: the ether intoxicates me, clears my mind, liberates endorphins. Something lifts me above myself. The mountain streams that bellow and overflow their banks invigorate me. I feel like I'm home. Without thinking about it, I divide the world in two: on the one hand, low valleys, and on the other, sparkling heights that lead me to a process of purification. The snow is first and foremost an eraser that wipes away the ugliness of the world, even if ugliness ends up triumphing in the end. Freshly fallen slow is miraculous: it buries the landscape, takes the edge off fences and posts, darkens contours, raises roofs and cornices above their normal levels. It has a very indiscreet way of infiltrating all the places it's not invited and taking up residence there. The structure of the flake, round, thin, angled, embodies the richness of what is infinitely small. If the sun rises after a night of snowfall, we're witness to the marvel of the first morning, one that shines and sparkles as though the landscape had been lacquered. Whirlwinds of white dust in shining fantasy worlds burn the eyes and dissolve in halos of light. It's a finely coated universe that squeaks beneath one's feet, immobile in the iron fist of the cold. The trees are donned in a thick fur of powder; sombre whispers course through the immense forest that suddenly seems neutralized. The mountains are draped as if for a great procession. The ice is at once a painter and a weaver: it sprinkles the trees with powder and traces a web of frost on the stones and the vegetation. The fields undulate and become expanses of meringue. The blanket of silk calls out to skis, asking them to profane it with their lovely looping traces. As we glide along, we believe ourselves capable of dancing at the surface of things, of transforming slopes into long, smooth ribbons. Falls are weightless, blunted by the thickness of the layer of snow. We come across the hieroglyphs of a chamois or a fox. We take ourselves for elves who are able to scale walls, and for whom the laws of gravity cease to exist. In our weightless state, we liquefy matter; our only soundtrack is the rustle of the tips of our skis.

If we go a little higher, the mountains seem to be coated in candied sugar, like the mountain hut at the dome of the Goûter that a telescope image taken in February 2021 showed literally embossed with several layers of crystals. The lace of such summits, with its cones, pyramids, and puffs, gives forth an entire *pâtisserie* of cold. The white landscape blinds the one who contemplates it; the light carves the peaks with all the details of a sculpture. So strong are the ultraviolet rays and the glare above 3,000 metres that the snow becomes incandescent. The telephone poles appear varnished, and bristle with little fingers of ice. It's an entire jewellery store that must be grasped the moment it appears, for it will soon be gone. Window panes, streaked with ice, trace geometrical enigmas. The snow is a shroud – a glorious shroud that enchants what it hides. But scarcely has this fleeting miracle come about than the warmth of the day returns, and the beautiful mounds melt, deflating like soufflés; the fragile porcelain of the landscape cracks, the stalactites drip as though they had a cold, and rivulets stream from the roofs. The sun shines upon the frozen shell, and what was pure and immaculate vanishes.

I remember my excitement the first time I was caught in a snowstorm, on the border between Germany and Austria. I was seven or eight years old, and we were travelling from Lyon, where my parents had settled, to the Kleinwalsertal, where we would spend Christmas. Several vehicles had slid into the ditch, and our little 4CVwas having trouble on the steep climb. It was impossible to distinguish the road from the fields: a single white covering erased the borders between them. We had to undertake the long ascent to get from the city of Oberstdorf, in Bavaria, to the village of Riezlern, in Austria. The 4CV was sliding all over the road, and wound up in a snowdrift as high as a wall, along with other vehicles that were sideways on the highway. My panicked mother pleaded with my father to turn back toward Lake Constance. I should say that I was my mother's little treasure, and that her love gave me a feeling of indestructible strength, even if she did tend to coddle me. The most difficult thing for an only child is to wean himself from the maternal embrace; the most difficult thing for a mother is to let her child go: both undergo a feeling of being wrenched away, but it's more difficult for the one who remains and who will never again have this unique feeling of fusion, while the little cherub goes off to wander and frolic. The car refused to go forwards or backwards. We had all been marooned, and we'd have to wait in the cold until morning, when the heaven-sent snowplough and tractor would come to drag us up to the border post. In the meantime, I'd fallen asleep on my mother's lap, my visions of the discontinuous curtain of flakes having on me the effect of a drug. I swore to myself that one day I'd live under this element's majestic reign.

Snow doesn't really fall. It sometimes seems to gush forth from the ground, defying the laws of gravity, scrambling our sense of direction, inverting high and low. Like a waterfall that, with the wind's effect, seems to climb back up toward its source and push the river back to its origin. This downy substance unfolds in curls, climbing toward the sky in an effort to coat it. It's breath-taking, and makes us feel as though we'll be swept away like a wisp of straw. A blizzard can annihilate the landscape in the blink of an eye, rendering it unrecognizable and disorienting its inhabitants. Every time I'm blocked in by snow, which sometimes happens in the Alps or in North America, I'm seized by a peculiar euphoria, almost a trance. I remember long January walks beneath gusts of wind in Montreal, Moscow, and New York: it was as though a furious hand was forcing icy seeds into my throat and eyes. I was coated by flakes as if by flour, suffocating with a clown's makeup on my face, my eyebrows pressed down by ice, my lips blue, my nose mottled, my nostrils blocked. The snow is an eruption of sharp projectiles that rush toward you horizontally, forcing a path through your lips, working their way into your mouth like sand. Granules of buckshot at point-blank range. You swim in an ocean of white that devours streets and avenues, attacks buildings, piles up in drifts, and sculpts tormented figures on telephone poles. Even though I've never been in desperate situations at 3,000 or 4,000 metres, where my mouth begins to freeze and I stop being able to feel my extremities, it seems to me that the howling of a snowstorm is less dangerous than that of a thunderstorm. In a snowstorm, you have the marvellous sensation of being cut off from the world, lost in a bubble far from human concerns. Passers-by are like ghosts in the mist; daylight fades away in a pallid dusk. In the distance you hear the melancholy cry of a groomer or a snowplough, with their multi-coloured blinking lights. As a rule, everything that disturbs the everyday reality of mortals delights me: polar temperatures, the sharpness of the cold, and ice that forms on sidewalks in slippery, viscous trails, forcing people into the delicate movements of a tightrope walker.

The whole charm of winter comes from the muted, hushed sensation that the snow brings about, and that gives rise to cosiness. Snow generally falls in a very gentle way: it's a noiseless noise made up of a thousand indistinct murmurs. The crystals crackle as they land. Falling snow is like the pallid whispering of words sent down to us from the sky. It adds to the feeling we already get in the mountains, that of being sequestered, and makes climbing all the more impracticable. A new land arises from this welcome storm: the sunken land. While we watch the snow fall, we think of the novel written by the German-Moldavian writer, Stefan Heyder Pontescu, entitled *The Little Dead Language*. In a high-elevation principality in the heart of Europe, in the middle of a remote and impenetrable mountain range, cut off from the world by the snow for six months of the year, a young princess is dying. A magician assures her father that she will be healed if she is able to see the sea when she gets out of bed. 'These horrible protuberances weigh on her soul and make her ill.' But her condition makes travel difficult, if not impossible. So the prince decides to have all the peaks separating his kingdom from the distant sea razed, for hundreds of kilometres. Thus begins the considerable task, one that mobilizes the entire lifeblood of the kingdom. They blow up the first few summits of the range separating the country from its neighbours to the south. In their haste, they overlook safety measures: workers die by the dozen in rock slides, as mountains take their revenge by falling on men. The entire population comes together to save the child, joining in to bring down the cursed mountains. All that can be heard is the noise of pickaxes, bulldozers, dynamite. The debris is piled hurriedly on the only plain of the country, forming a large hill in its own right. Night and day, people live in a cloud of dust that blocks the nasal passages of children, who cough and cry to bring life back to the little princess. When, at the end of five months, the peaks that blocked the view of the sea have all been razed, the workers see an immense lake in the distance whose vast size makes it seem like an ocean, and on which sailboats move about gracefully. Only a single rocky rise still blocks the horizon. Time is short: the princess's condition is worsening. Everyone gets to work: the king promises huge bonuses to whoever is the first to destroy the obstacle. The last forests are brought down; trenches are dug in the fields of snow; glaciers are cleared; peaks are transformed into hills, hills into rises, and rises into bumps, which are then flattened. Finally, one night, the last proud mound of the chain crumbles in a horrific din. In the morning, the landscape is unrecognizable, and in the distance, beyond the still-smoking ruins, shining like an eye on the earth, appears the shimmering surface of a great expanse of water. The child is brought to the top of the castle's highest tower, and with an astronomer's telescope she is shown the sea, its beaches, its boats. She smiles in ecstasy, lets out a sob, and dies.

I've just turned fifteen, and my relationship with my father is awful: he wants to impose his ideas upon me, he yells at my mother, he hits her. I sometimes hope with all my heart that he dies. Our fathers, born between the two world wars, were already crackpot patriarchs, unsure of themselves, who used violence to compensate for their loss of power, which future generations would continue to undermine. To patch up our tense relationship, he invites me to go skiing on May 1st: the plan is to travel from Lyon to Courchevel, to take advantage of an exceptionally large snowfall. We leave very early and arrive just when the ski lifts are opening. In the middle of the 1960s, Courchevel is still a small village without tower blocks, oligarchs, or charters bringing in prostitutes. The snow is soft at the base of the mountain, barely more than water, but the higher we get, the firmer it becomes. The ski resort will be closing tomorrow. My dad's a decent skier, but I make up for my lack of technique by skiing faster. I pass him and leave him far behind, thus taking a puerile revenge: I use my youth to repudiate him. We're enchanted, but also sunburned: my mother had slid some sunscreen into my pocket, but I made it a point of honour not to use it, and that evening she's met with two cooked, copper-coloured faces. The same year, at Christmas, I return with some friends to Courchevel, where we stay in a youth hostel. One evening, my heart beating furiously, I gaze at a beautiful blond who never looks in my direction. She literally looks right through me, and my misery is complete when I see an 'old' guy of twenty, with broad shoulders and a voice long broken, walk up to her, make her laugh, and accompany her outside to keep flirting. The soundtrack for my humiliation is the Beatles' song 'A Hard Day's Night', which is being played again and again and which, since then, I've associated with that moment of mute, nonreciprocal ecstasy. Twenty years later, I'm skiing with my son at La Plagne. He's fantastic, taking risk after risk on the descent and then turning around, exasperated by my slowness. I'm only thirty-five, but he has all the audacity and fearlessness that I've lost. The tables have turned: I've become the cautious man I used to mock.

Thirty years later, in 2012, I spend three days at Méribel ski resort with my fifteen-year-old daughter. It's March 22nd, the first day of spring. It's warm, too warm: the snow has already turned to soup at the bottom of the mountain, and we have to go up to the Caron peak, above 3,000 metres, to find nice powder. Lunch – *crozets* or *tartiflette au soleil* – makes for a fantastic moment in a sublime décor, and we end each meal with a little glass of Génépi, to give ourselves conviction for the slopes. But as soon as we get below 2,000 metres we're swimming in puddles where grass and rocks are already showing. Exhausted by the thick snow, I stop, while my daughter continues. The slightly granular sugar of snow that has melted and then frozen once more gives way to a syrup that sticks to the tips of your skis, a grey and muddy stew. In the last sixty years, winter has shortened by a month, with the exception of rare cold years now and again. To ski is to go back and forth between the euphoria of caresses and the defiance of harshness – between sliding effortlessly and forcing it, taking the risk of stumbling and, eventually, flailing about like a beetle turned onto its back. You never feel quite as defeated as when you collapse in front of someone you're trying to impress, who then gracefully goes past you. But I try to remain faithful to the rituals of my childhood: skiing every year, even if only for a few days, and never stopping once I'm going downhill, even if it means snowploughing when things get difficult.

My mountain is intimate, modest, sweet. I love its peaceful beauty, its laughing colours. It is first and foremost a sentimental landscape of high and inviting fertile valleys, of dells covered in beautiful snow. It's a place covered in small villages where you spend time in chalets with family or friends in a festive and joyful ambiance. And even if I climb a bit higher during the summer, I don't take myself for an eagle, even less for a chamois – only a being whose weight has been temporarily taken away. I don't have the superiority complex that tarnishes mountaineering, often turning it into a virility contest. Climbing schools and mountain huts alike ooze testosterone. The monarchic contemplation of the world that Bachelard speaks about leaves me cold. I like raising my eyes to the sky when I reach a peak, not looking at what is down below. The land of on high, with its terraces that rise progressively up to the level of glaciers and screes, is a precious land, a rare land. Today snow has become parsimonious, and at times plays a mean trick on us by staying away until February and then appearing like a kind of magical plunder. Its arrival is like a radiance that causes colours to alter. 'Where Goes the White When Melts the Snow?' runs a question often attributed to Shakespeare. It goes into the earth, which soaks it up like a sponge and pours it out into streams and rivers. Where go the turned pages during the reading of a book? Which ones carry consequences, which ones fall into the great pit of forgetting? How many novels have reverberated within us, and how many have disappeared without a trace? For the last few years, low-altitude ski resorts have begun to resemble those village weddings that are prepared far in advance: the sporting goods stores are ready, the ski lifts are oiled, their bolts tightened and checked, ski instructors stand at attention, vacation-goers come in droves. All that's missing is the bride – the snow, who makes everyone wait, and whose arrival everyone watches out for: will those flakes that are light as a chicka-dee's feet deign to come down to our level? These towns look like bald heads with a few pale stains here and there on their northern slopes.

These days, we view snow as a vestige of the past, so much so that when we get heavy snowfalls, we think an error has occurred, some sort of archaic weather. Didn't a British journalist claim in 2010 that England would never again witness snowfalls? A few years later, the entire country was shut down by snow. Falling snow is no longer a winter routine – it's a gift from the gods, and we should treat it as such. In spring we wait to see it transformed into something akin to a carpet, crimped like drooping cream, undulated by the wind. You can't drink snow any more than you can drink sea water, for it is shot through with particles that aren't fit to be consumed. Is there anything more enjoyable than when, during a summer descent, you can slide down firns on the seat of your pants, using your ice axe as a brake?

I also remember the cold winters – frozen pipes, cars stuck in the snow – and I've observed the change that has taken place. Winters in the past were far more generous than those of today: snow was counted in metres; it piled up into high walls that kept you from opening your door. In the mountains, it built ramparts around cabins – you entered through the second-floor windows; the roof sagged beneath its weight, and you had to shovel for hours to unblock the door. It was the magic of an enormous concealment. For weeks, the world became a spectre drowned in shadows. The snow would generally stop around lunchtime, only to begin its chorus once more in the afternoon. It pierced the landscape with thousands of petals, like so many lilies drooping down to the ground. The mountain became a cushion, a quilt beneath which everyone could rest; it seemed to be crouching, set down upon its backside. Its shining whiteness purified us from within.

I recall that during the glacial winter of 1956–57, when I was eight, my parents told me that the septic tank was at risk of exploding because of the ice. I wasn't even aware of its existence, but I discovered both its reality and our shame on the same day. A vacuum truck came the next morning, preceded by an unflattering odour. It was a delicate operation: they had to thaw everything out before digging, which meant heating it little by little with a blowtorch before sucking it up. The driver and his assistant, both wearing masks, opened this devil's hole as wide as they could and set about trying to unfreeze everything. Horrendous odours, carried by the cold air, soon invaded the house. I didn't know where to go to get away from them. I was disgusted, but I also wanted to see what was happening. I imagined the cistern rising up and covering us in the dishonour of our own excretions. With each passing moment, I awaited the revolt from below, the eruption of the caca volcano that would sully the countryside, covered in snow. My father, acting as the great orchestrator of our absolution, directed the operations. In the early afternoon, they were able to begin draining the tank, its contents returned to their liquid state. At five o'clock, the vacuum truck departed, filled with the weight of our refuse. My father gave the chilled workers something to drink and rewarded them handsomely. Our sins having been absolved, the house was healthy once more, rid of the putrid lake floating beneath its foundation. It was like a purification of our souls.

Since my childhood, I've lived a life within strict limits: medium-sized mountains surrounded by peaks, forests that closely watched over me, the soothing symphony of cowbells, the limpid cascades of mountain streams, cabins that seem as tiny as dollhouses in the immensity of the environment. I love these closed-off, uterine spaces, idyllic in the extreme. The smaller the bedroom – with its bed built into the wall like a boat's cabin – the happier I am. This claustrophobia enchants me. A chalet – even one that is now inhabited by tourists rather than farmers – embodies a sober opulence in which every inch of space is calculated to resist cold weather and storms. It exemplifies a sumptuous modesty, and this is all the more true of A-frame chalets, those structures that look like tepees that get smaller the higher up you go. Every square metre has a function. The only luxuries that can be seen are the sculpted lintels, the canopy beds in some of the rooms, and the flowers on the balcony railings during the summer, which fall in cascades of colours. The chalet is the triumph of confined life. 'I dread winter because it is the season of comfort',[4] said Rimbaud. 'I've caught winter', a Romantic poet once lamented, referring at once to his cold and the melancholy of his soul. For me, it's the reverse: I love winter because it is the moment of warm seclusion with loved ones and good books. I love classic Christmases spent around a tree, with carols in German when possible. I'm not a believer, but culturally I remain a Christian, out of loyalty to my childhood. At Christmastime I'm like an old cat who purrs on the radiator and allows himself to be petted. I'm drawn to the unknown, but I can only approach it if I have a refuge, a sort of home base. Rather than providing an extravagant amount of space, a chalet seems to fit snugly to the human body, with its small spaces, low ceiling, and blackened panels around the fireplace. Above the door, there's often an inscription in Latin that commends one's soul to God, or deals with the brevity of life and the necessity of hospitality. The chalet is both cradle and tomb: it is life brought to its most basic state, the nestled existence of marmots, chests full of food and clothing, rustic and comforting tables of thick wood, with an adjoining shelter where logs, hay, and salted meats are piled up. And stairs or a ladder leading to the attic; the tenderness of the wooden beams – oak, cedar, pine, or spruce – that breathe and live alongside the humans. And, until not so long ago, above all in Switzerland and Austria, great cast iron or earthenware wood burners, covered in naive paintings of a precious sophistication, around which we all huddled. Wood is hard and knotted, but this nodosity protects us: it has a memory and a warmth, as opposed to concrete, which expresses only its own stupid consistency. The chalet is life in miniature, which is why certain mountain landscapes recall the world of toys, a perfect illustration of which is Switzerland, with its little rack-and-pinion trains that nibble away at the slopes, runner sleds (the scooters of high altitudes), villages perched on mountainsides, extravagant hotels at 2,000 or 3,000 metres. In order to survive, people have to huddle up and do battle against the inhuman grandeur of the summits. In my imagination, Savoy, Switzerland, both Tyrols, and the Aosta Valley are toy countries that have brought nature's savagery down to the dimensions of a child's room. Farms, which used to be synonymous with poverty and parsimony – people lived side by side with their herds – have become expensive toys for city dwellers. Rustic discomfort has been converted into luxury, to the point that nowadays it's common to build fake lodgings for millionaires, complete with artificially aged logs.

In January 1867, Émile Zola published a lovely article on the arrival of snow in Paris, admitting that he felt 'joyous in the silliest of ways'. Winter has given a marvellous gift to the city, bestowing upon it a 'pure and unsullied carpet'. The streets have become 'wide bands of white satin', while the branches of trees are covered by 'a light garnishing of lace'. Since that time, there has been less and less snow in Paris, and what does fall remains for only a few hours. The concrete turns white, the world is transformed, and adults and children alike spontaneously recover their feeling for life. Snowball fights, sleigh rides, and even – as we saw in January 2021 – descents of the Montmartre hill on skis for those who are daring, with plenty of falls on the turns. Snow is joy: it lifts the soul above its normal state. But greyness quickly returns: the alabaster crown turns into muddy streams that are like so many scars, sullying purity and destroying radiance. Why does the whiteness of snow give such joy to people of all ages? It is an elixir of youth, a tangible light that you can eat, form into different shapes, inhabit; above all, you can slide upon it. Snow is a solid colour that falls upon the earth to illuminate it. And that turns to liquid in your hand the moment you touch it. The entire sky participates in this miracle, in this blurry lucidity. In Madrid, the January 2021 storm that was given the lovely name Filomena shut down the capital for a week, with deep snowdrifts and temperatures of minus 10 Celsius. It was like a long, pearly recess that forced the city's shivering residents to dress up as skiers, tobogganers, snowshoers, and trappers. The springtime melting of snow is another kind of miracle: little fountains awake, rustle, chatter; crocuses peep out of the earth; the white carpet begins to chip and peel; frostbitten grass turns green once more; colours return after a long purgatory. Emaciated marmots poke their muzzles out of their burrows, and bears remember that the day exists. It is a rebirth after a period of general lethargy.

When the snow falls, our eyes slowly close: this continuous and almost hypnotic fall plunges us into a retinal torpor, a wilful narcosis. Which allows us to better understand the temptation of lost mountaineers and exhausted hikers to lie down and close their eyes in the warmth of this quilt that erases trails and memory alike. It's a fatal lethargy. To die in the snow is to end your days in a white, frozen happiness. Only snow abolishes the thin line of demarcation between life and death, sleep and eternity, exhaustion and resurrection.

CHAPTER 2

# Why Climb?

When you climb the stairs, you're always more tired at the end than at the beginning. Given that this is the case, shouldn't we begin every climb with the last steps, and end with the first?

PIERRE DAC

Everyone who climbs toward a summit, weighed down by a heavy pack, asks herself sooner or later: what am I doing here? Hanging from a rock face, with nothing but the void beneath, hurried along by other climbers, she thinks to herself: what's the use of all this difficulty if all I'm going to do is climb back down after a brief pause at the summit? Is this fleeting moment of grace really worth all the effort? It's comforting to know that the greatest climbers have asked themselves the same question. In 1983, at the summit of Cho Oyu (an 8,188-metre mountain in the Himalayas) alongside Reinhold Messner and Michael Dacher, a certain Hans Kammerlander, in an absolutely desperate state, stammered: 'What was the point of coming here?'[1] The answer is complicated, and any explanation based on an all-powerful ego is insufficient. A prideful being does not put himself in a state of quasi-agony – at least, not unless his eventual reward will compensate for all the pain he has experienced, unless his desire for the peak is more important to him than the sacrifices he will assent to. The possibility of death becomes preferable to survival: this is the great mystery of it all. Mountains are perfect illustrations of the delicious absurdity of existence: we're only born to die one day; our lives are brief intervals preceded and followed by nothingness; we climb in order to descend. The only difference is that we know only one life, but we climb many mountains. It's not Sisyphus who pushes his rock to the top of the hill, it's the rock that pushes Sisyphus to climb again and again. We should imagine a happy Sisyphus, said Camus. To which Valéry responded: we should imagine a Sisyphus with big muscles.

There's something all climbers know: hoisting yourself to the top of a mountain (or even a little hill), looking around and seeing cliff walls bathed in turquoise and bright pink, watching valleys emerge from the shadows, and seeing the sun rise into the sky – all of this is an immense joy. It's the simple joy of reaching your limits. This is the paradox of every climb: you exhaust yourself to enlarge yourself. Tenacity turns into rapture. Who wouldn't accept a few blisters and cramps to defy the laws of gravity? When the entire world has already been photographed, climbing above it means frustrating the dominance of the eye. Seeing is easy – climbing is subtle. 'Lead your body toward those places where seeing happens for the first time', as Gaston Rebuffat said. If humans have a desire to explore, it's above all so as to do something eventful, even if only in a modest way, rather than being reduced to the role of spectator. I know of no more intense joy than that of using the pads of my fingers and my torso to commune with stone, and using my legs to commune with slopes. It can be difficult to bear, but there's a joy in bearing, in sweating, in backbreaking effort. Taking on a peak, with all the retreats, the stops and starts, circumventions, and tricks that this entails, all of which lead toward a prudent yet ecstatic final climb to the summit, is above all a victory against yourself and against uniformity.

The entire enigma of a mountain lies in the way it converts adversity into joy. You push up against your limits, and in doing so, you feel your strength. The resistance of the wall to your will makes it eminently desirable. Climbing is a form of asceticism. Your heart beating wildly, your lungs burning, your knees pushing toward their breaking point, fingernails torn through constant scraping – all of this makes for a pain that is full of meaning, because it is directed toward a goal. These experiences form the fate and even the stigmata of the ordinary climber. They result in a fatigue that is marked with love, a knowledge obtained by way of the muscles. The ordeal strengthens us in those moments when rest would weaken us. An ascent without hardship would be nothing more than a little nature walk. To climb is to enter another dimension, even for an amateur like me. Tolerance for filth, and indifference to a lack of privacy and discomfort, are offset by the certainty of feeling active. Scars work the body of the climber like a crucifixion, but a voluntary one – it's the price you pay to not spend all day sitting on your butt.

There are two kinds of suffering: the one you endure, and the one you choose; the one that afflicts you, and the one that transforms you. Nothing important is ever achieved without torment. You have to manage the rhythm of feet squeezed into boots, take your blisters and your aching tendons into account: this is small change for a will that finds joy in exerting itself and going beyond itself. At altitude, well-being is indistinguishable from that which hinders it; we end up taking delight in what had at first caused us all sorts of pain. In the midst of total exhaustion, we find within ourselves what we need to get out of a jam, to overcome difficulty: every great mountaineering narrative includes these moments of miraculous recovery. There's a sweetness to pain: the ascent doesn't feel real if it doesn't leave me gasping for air as I nurse my sore knees. Too much ease would be miserable, while too much difficulty would be pointless. Regeneration takes place through a total demolition of the body. The mountain gets inside you through your legs, your back, your torso. It's a discipline in the best sense of the term. You have to put yourself on the line, as they say. Why should you abuse your body this way? Because the body only revels in difficulty: it even seeks hardship in big hills. Pleasure derived from extreme struggle is superior to that of leisure. Few things give a greater sense of achievement than reaching the top of a tough ascent. Descending back down to the plain after two or three days at altitude, by way of an endless trail with switchbacks and detours, seeing the bluish mist rising from the valley, slowly discerning the outlines of chalets in the intense green of the prairie – all of this is an incomparable joy. You're at once exhausted and jubilant: you feel more glorious than a king. The mountain is my delight and my remedy.

I'm not a mountaineer who writes, or even 'a writer who mountaineers', as Paul Yonnet once said; I'm a walker who hangs about on summits. I've returned to being a mountain dweller belatedly, after a childhood spent at high altitudes. I did a bit of rock climbing in the Oisans region of the Alps when I was a teenager. Being reinitiated into climbing around the age of forty – by my friend Laurent Aublin, who has since passed away – has made me feel like a soldier engaging in a war against time that is lost in advance. Still, it's worth it: you don't climb to succeed, but to continue to climb. The former German chancellor Helmut Kohl used to speak about the grace that he'd experienced, that of being born too late – too late to be enlisted by the Nazis (we know that in fact he lied a little about the dates). But how to speak of the grace of a belated revelation that comes about during a time of life when you're supposed to be slowing down? It's never too late to dive headlong into impossible challenges. You just have to give up those goals that are out of reach – adjust your objectives, in other words, to your abilities. Whether you're twenty or seventy, you're going to feel a tingling sensation when you're standing at the foot of the highest mountains. But it's true that your legs become uncertain and your joints squeak as you age. Hiking in the mountains is a form of voluntary servitude in which you attach the yoke yourself, because it allows you to strengthen your friendship with the world. I grew up on a gentle mountain, and I've always feared those that are more hostile. And yet even as they repel me, these hostile mountains also attract me, due to a puerile need to enlarge my life in the face of that which negates it.

The skier climbs to descend, but the climber descends to climb back up. These activities belong to two entirely different realms. The virgin expanse of a valley or a firn, after several hours of climbing in ski skins, is a mute apostrophe that says to you: descend me if you can. The frozen quilt commands me to leave beautiful parallel lines in my wake. The tips of my skis swallow up the space before me, mocking the bumps and hollows I encounter, encountering no resistance at all. The snowy covering that smooths out the surface gives a false impression that the danger has been lessened – that you can laugh at obstacles, narrow passageways, vertiginous slopes. The only hard thing is to get going, since seeing it all from the top can be daunting. I admire the grace and elegance of those heroes of extreme skiing, the precision of their vertical choreography – 'Anything white can be descended', in the words of Anselme Baud – but their exploits are beyond me. Just thinking about what they do numbs me with terror. They make the world seem unreal, jostling the borders of space and time: they're shooting stars on boards, free riders who become birds, able to dance in the void and to sail above rocky ridges. They at once use and efface their bodies, defying the logic of gravity and liquefying all that is solid. They've become weightless; they glide, disencumbered from themselves; in the speed with which they brush past any possible obstacle, they quash both inertia and rough surfaces. They construct an utter utopia in their evasion of gravity.

You can't cheat in the mountains: standing at the base of a wall, at the bottom of a steep climb, you're naked. You confront the hardest trial there is: the trial of the self. I've known many boastful men who have backed down when the moment of this trial arrived. For the climber, each summit is like Warhol's fifteen minutes of fame. But the only way to advance is to admit your weakness, and to limit yourself to minor objectives. You have to find your own experience of the infinite: that little path that shrinks to a line of dust, that overhang beneath its lichen moss, that crack into which you'd like to sink but that you have to cross whatever the cost and in spite of your fear. But there's also wisdom in knowing when to quit, even if it means you'll have to start over later on. All it takes is a cracked meniscus to turn an excellent climber into someone who can't move: this little pad that cushions and lubricates the knee produces shooting pains when aggravated and takes away our fundamental right to flexibility, as if it were saying to us: no bending allowed.

Why climb?[2] The best answer to this question was given by the Englishman George Mallory, who was asked why he wanted to ascend Everest: 'Because it's there!' This is a more complex turn of phrase than it seems. George Mallory was haunted and even obsessed by Everest: he scouted the mountain twice, in 1921 and 1922, before dying on it in 1924, at the age of thirty-seven, along with his companion, Andrew Irvine. There is no proof that they reached the summit, but as a result of Mallory's legend, a great many people have sought to follow in his footsteps. His body was even found, perfectly conserved and mummified at 8,300 metres, on May 1st, 1999, seventy-five years after he disappeared. You climb to escape a life lived horizontally, on flat plains; you climb because you want to imitate, and share the passion of, those who climbed before you. You fall in love with a mountain before beginning its ascension: you repeat its name, you follow its paths on a map or a screen, you study it, you savour it, you scrutinize the tough parts of the climb, you look forward to arriving at the summit and turning back like a lover before an intimate encounter. What do you learn in the high country? You gain insight into your vulnerability and your strength. I love mountains because only a mountain – not the sea, not the countryside – makes me feel that I really have a body. To endure hardships on trails and rock faces is to be alive. You learn how to tune out the pinching of your vertebrae; you learn to push yourself until you collapse and then to return transformed from this journey to the limits of your ability. You regard the assembly of lofty peaks as so many crowned heads looking down and weighing you up. And then you take up the challenge. The ascent is an almost religious activity: as Robert Macfarlane said, there is no mountain but that of the mind.[3]

The high mountains are the kingdom of malevolent invisibility. In the morning, a deceptive sun makes you think you're in for a calm day, but by noon, dreadful puffy clouds cover the peaks. It's the triumph of the U-turn: in less than an hour, an idyllic scene can become a nightmare. The luminous sky takes on a deathly pallor, while the slopes take on the colour of kraft paper. You have to depart these chimeric expanses immediately. The beautiful view was deceptive, a peaceful interval between squalls. When the storm hits, it's panic. I remember a terrifying descent in the Écrins range, from a hut that lay at almost 3,000 metres. There were about twenty of us running terrified from the unleashed elements as though we were deserters fleeing a bombardment. Each of us was an ideal target for the lightning; I selfishly told myself that I had only a five per cent chance of being struck. At every moment I imagined one of the deserters falling beside me. Certain of them – those with extra weight or bad footwear – did indeed fall, and we had to stop and help them up. With every thunderclap I hunched my shoulders dreading the possibility of electrocution. Avalanches of rocks shattered the slopes across the valley with a great roar. I thought of all the signs of imminent lightning strikes with which mountaineers are acquainted: creaking ice axes, the humming of swarms of bees, the abhorrent smell of sulphur. I arrived at the bottom an hour later, soaking wet, almost disappointed at not having been singled out by the fury of the elements.

We don't know what a body can do, as Spinoza said. His phrase has been ruminated upon many times. But there's a different law that you learn in middle age: you can only fight fatigue with more fatigue. It's an error to think that rest will compensate us for all the hardships of existence. 'I'm running headlong toward destruction – in other words, my destruction will arrive the moment I stop running', in the magnificent formulation of the Italian philosopher Norberto Bobbio. Climbing is a humble way of relearning this empirical truth: there's more to us than we think. Our muscles, our heart, and our lungs are amazed to have such abundance at their disposal. Even at an advanced age, our old carcasses still assert themselves, brimming with power and confidence. A new body – one we didn't know we had – is born from the old one, and we're surprised by the delight and the effort of which it is capable. Even at the age of seventy, we can be bowled over by incredible pleasure, and achieve superhuman feats. Sometimes you have to wear yourself out to arrive at a superior degree of energy, bringing your muscles to such extremes that they find their true power. Mountains expand us; on the best days, they even raise us above ourselves. For Spinoza, to return to him, joy is everything that increases the ability to act, while sadness is anything that diminishes it. It's the body's energy that makes the mind capable of great things. This involves a delicate balance: if you push the body too much, you can exhaust it under its own weight; if you don't push it enough, you might weaken it. It's an instrument that needs to be forced to its limits from time to time. It's the body that makes the rules, for a knight is powerless without his horse. Getting older means learning how to save your strength, but only so that you can use it more effectively when you need to. This allows you not to give up on your desires, regardless of how impossible they may seem, and mountains are one such desire for those who love them. Ageing is like walking down a long hallway whose doors close one after the other. The challenge is keeping at least one of them open as long as possible before darkness sets in. It always encourages me to see people in their eighties scaling walls at dizzying heights. Doesn't Marcel Rémy, a former railway worker who became a passionate mountaineer, work out on a climbing wall every week at the age of ninety-eight, studying each passage as though he were solving a puzzle? He has no intention of stopping.

We should admit that it's often pride that drives a climber – after all, life sometimes consists in turning flaws into virtues. On an August morning sixteen years ago, climbing with a few friends from the Izoard pass to the Rochebrune peak (3,325 metres) in the Queyras, we arrived, after four hours, to within 100 metres of the summit (having putting in a huge effort to cross an immense scree), in the light of the moon. When you're at altitude, the mountains that are farthest in the distance seem to get closer, while those that are closer seem farther away. Our sense of distance is distorted, as though the kilometres of space were filtered through a spatial accordion that extended or shortened them at will. You think you've arrived, but there's still one more slope to descend, one more stream to ford, one more valley to cross before you reach your destination. My companions, all seasoned mountaineers, began to climb the long, steep chimney separating us from the summit – one last rocky outcrop before we reached our goal. I was intimidated, and decided to let them go ahead, thinking I'd done enough and not feeling able to go any higher. At which point a middle-aged man arrived, said hi, recognized me, and asked in a surprised voice:

'Are you stopping here?'

'No, of course not, I was just admiring the view.'

'It's even nicer from the summit!'

He'd barely spoken, and already I was starting through the narrow passageway, which was blocked, I believe, by a large rock, and which led, fifteen minutes later, to the summit's crest, its sublime panorama rewarding my effort. Only the fear of seeming like a coward had kept me going. There are only a few times I've had to turn around on a climb, and they still stick in my craw. How many times, in the middle of a difficult ascent, have I burned with the desire to turn back? Didn't I continue each and every time so as not to seem like a failure to others? I'm always scared at the foot of a climb, whether of a steep wall, the sharp edge of a narrow ridge, a high crossing – any of these is enough to paralyse me. I don't know what prevails in me at these moments, whether it's fear of being ridiculed or fear, full stop. I go limp like a rag doll: my legs wobble, I lose my composure. Only pride keeps me going: I offset my panic by the desire to return to the base of the mountain carefree, with my head held high. If anyone finds this ludicrous, too bad.

How can a heap of rocks become an object of passion? In fact, the whole question of aesthetic feeling has been wrapped up in this since the Enlightenment. For centuries, no one dreamed of climbing or admiring mountaintops, unless it was to extract rock crystal or silver, taking whatever meagre harvest one could. Only shepherds, hunters, bootleggers, and those who were destitute lived in these fearful and wretched places. It's true that a few brave souls scaled mountains – Petrarch went up Ventoux in 1336, and the knight Antoine de Ville climbed Mount Aiguille in the Vercors, on the orders of Charles VIII, then king of France, in 1492 – but an entire shift in sensibility was required before these horrible mountains came to be viewed, at the end of the *ancien régime*, in a positive light. The migration toward mountains will probably double over the course of this century in a context of hot summers and the overpopulation of coastal regions.

Why climb? Because the mountain calls out to us: certain ranges and certain chains are invitations to get lost in them, to roam through them. A call for what? The mountains don't tell us. But there is perhaps a message to decipher in the compact indifference of their stone. When we're far from them, we feel – whether we're right or wrong – as if we've shrunk. They encourage us as much as they intimidate us. What is at stake is truly an *elevation* in the religious sense of the word. The mountain doesn't descend toward us so as to be at our level. On the contrary, it consents to our invasion of it without losing anything of its grandeur. The permission it grants us is temporary, and can always be revoked.

The important thing is to have the passion – a raging desire to climb. The ever-changing landscape and the endless views are the reward for the effort. There's a delight in looking down and seeing the path you've taken to the top. Everything looks different: the little lake you passed a while ago, the hut nestled between two blocks of stone, the entire difficult passage now seems unthreatening. Genre painting, photography, and satellite images have all detracted from our ability to be surprised by what we perceive. But it's enough to go from looking at mountains to experiencing them to understand the difference. We climb to open our souls to the celestial realm. Every ascent is both material and spiritual: *The mountain is another region of being. The mineral form of transcendence.* Its silences, the poetry of its wilderness, and the communion we feel with its landscapes allow us to enlarge and enrich our capacity for joy. It responds to the old revolutionary dream of luxury for all, of beauty for the humblest among us. Luxury today resides in everything that is becoming rare: untouched spaces, slow movement, meditation, the pleasure of being outside of time, the enjoyment of great works, the life of the mind – so many privileges that can't be bought, that are literally priceless.

Being a man of passion is superior to being a man of curiosity: curiosity cuts across us, but passion possesses us. It gives you a reason to live: dilettantes may flit around, but passion anchors you in the world that you share with others. 'Happiness consists in having many passions and many ways to gratify those passions', said the utopian philosopher Charles Fourier. I've only ever been excited by simple things: books, poetry, carnal pleasure, travel, and mountains. The question of whether one walks in order to walk or in order to get somewhere is one of the greatest philosophical questions. Does the mountaineer climb to get exercise or to reach the summit? Obviously he needs a destination, one that he aims for with his climbing partners and that gives them a collective project. The summit is the psychological magnet that pulls them upward. Every step that brings them closer to it is a joyful one. To climb is to endure, but to do so with a reward awaiting you. Even Sisyphus, for whom movement is more important than the objective, reaches his goal in the end.

# CHAPTER 3

# Our Universal Mother

At our home we have a milk cow:
Our universe is not large enough for the milk she gives
Her dress is dark blue, her name: 'Horn of Plenty'
Her pasture is the immense world
She has no calf; she is ready
To become the mother of anyone.

TUKARAM, *PSAUMES DU PÈLERIN*, SEVENTEENTH CENTURY

The mountain is inhabited: you're never alone when you're there, and if you know how to look, you can see the 'little people' – our smaller brothers – everywhere around you. Among all this fauna is one creature that has always moved me: the cow. It has been my fetish animal since I was a child, first and foremost for a simple reason: I love to drink milk and I adore all of its mutations, such as heavy cream, yogurt, cheese, curds, ice cream, cottage cheese – an entire world of flavours that industry tries to standardize and sterilize. Until I was forty, I would order pasteurized milk in cafés, to the chagrin of waiters who would urge me to have a glass of red wine or a beer instead of this 'chick's drink'. I've been called a 'cow lover', a 'mama's boy', a 'breastfeeder', and other nice names. God knows I've tried to drink wine and liqueurs so I wouldn't stick out. I can't do it. Cigarettes are even worse: I tried to smoke for years to be like others. Since then, I've taken a stand: all I order is tea, like the old Englishwoman I've become. In France, not having a drink with your meal makes you a pariah, an anomaly, or the object of pity. People think of me as a gloomy puritan, to which I always respond: I don't keep my libido in a bottle of wine. The idea of the vegan sect replacing cow's milk with oat milk, barley milk, or almond milk – in other words, substituting chemical or industrial contrivances for nature – fills me with horror. For me, the culture of mountaineering goes hand in hand with the worship of warm, fresh milk that has just been taken from the teat – the liquid brother of snow with its hints of hazelnut, especially during the summer when the cows are brought up to mountain pastures, where they graze on bellflowers, buttercups, gentians, rhododendrons, and absent these, saxifrages and lichen. There ought to be milk tasters today, just as there were once water tasters. What could be more seductive than a bowl of this cool liquid with its iridescent depths that turns to gold at its first contact with the air, at the mere sight of which you can already taste the fruity flavours of a Beaufort, an Appenzeller, a Comté? Visiting a *fruiterie* (a 'fruit market', as artisanal cheese stalls in the Alps are called), especially one that is right beside a cowshed, means witnessing an entire cycle of rebirths: the hyper-white of milk in thick pastes, in wheels of cheese that are rolled and then stored for ripening. The soft tapestry of meadows has turned into soft and fragrant circles and rectangles. A cowshed at altitude is not a business; it is an oratory, an altar, the site of an almost biblical transmutation analogous to the nativity scene: the magical gift of the animal kingdom to humanity, the communion between every species. Milk is finally an ephemeral and corruptible product that alters with the warmth of its atmosphere: it thickens into lumps and takes on an odour that is at first merely unpleasant, but quickly becomes rank. The white gold turns back into lead.

How can we not be amazed by the recent demonization of milk, and of the cows that are held responsible for global warming because of the methane contained in their gases? It's a revival of the same polemic, with new arguments, that arose in 1954 with Pierre Mendès France's decision to give each schoolchild a glass of milk, which aroused the fury of the winegrowers' lobby. Mendès – whose detractors said the only thing French about him was his name – was dragged through the mud, in particular by Pierre Poujade. Today it's in the name of 'anti-speciesism' – the rejection of human domination over other species – that people want to cut all contact with the animal kingdom: think of the huge banner in the Lausanne train station that condemned cheesemaking and judged the farming of bovines to be a form of racist domination. By this reasoning, we should no longer milk cows, sentence them to die in extreme suffering, or have them disappear completely from the face of the earth. This is a strange way of showing solidarity.

Everything about a cow moves me: her damp, compassionate gaze, her long, fringed eyelashes, her moist nose, her spotted dress, her thick flanks, her fabulous body, and the relief of bluish veins on her teats. Even her dung is a sign of the regeneration of the earth. She's the universal mother who protects us. Even the bell she wears makes me quiver. When ruminants moo, shaking the bells hanging from their leather collars crafted with golden nails, it's as though the melody of mountain pastures were inflected in a new way – it's almost an animal symphony. If every animal is one note, then two notes make a sonata, and four an orchestra. Whenever we went to the farm during my childhood, we were allowed, one night per week, to set down a mattress near the cowshed and sleep in the warm smell of dung and milk. The livestock, sensing our presence, would move around, low, and share their flies with us. We were awoken at five o'clock for the milking, which wasn't yet mechanized, and were allowed to take part with our clumsy fingers, to pull on these hard and rubbery teats that resisted our attempts to draw milk from them. Even so, the contact with these mammals filled us with wonder.

We slander the cow by describing her as a placid beast who watches trains go by. In reality, she's the most industrious animal of all – a veritable Stakhanovite. She works tirelessly even when she's resting: she ruminates with her four stomachs, regurgitating and chewing her food about 40,000 times a day. All she asks is to be milked in the morning and the evening, to be relieved of that precious substance she bestows upon humanity. In Grand-Bornand, a naive sculpture presents her standing on her hind legs, her teats in the form of a fountain from which water gushes – she is the sacrificial animal par excellence. She's a marvellous factory in and of herself, a stomach held up by hooves. Her rough tongue often licks rock salt, those great blocks of yellow soap that are the heart of the alpine pastures. You see her balancing on steep terrain, willing to brave vertigo for a thick clump of grass. Don't let her good-natured appearance fool you: certain breeds of cow are aggressive. Having witnessed clashes between 'queens' in the Mont Blanc region and in the Val d'Hérens in Switzerland for the right to lead the herd up to pastures, I can testify to the power on display in these forehead-to-forehead scrums. These good mothers, beautifully decked out in impeccable silk dresses, made up and adorned for battle, are like young bulls, their necks coiled, their nostrils smoking, their rear hooves braced. The winner, with her fierce eyes and her dress soaked in sweat, receives the reward of having her horns decorated with ribbons – not to mention the submissiveness of the other cows.

This mammal is a hub of activity who never rests or takes time off: even when she sleeps, she produces milk. A poet should sing the praises of her ceaseless labour. And when a storm breaks, whether of rain or snow, she arches her back and persists in her work. Generally speaking, the animal world is no model of calm or serenity: animals, forced to fight to survive, to eat, and to escape predators, are paragons of hyperactivity. The squirrel eats with speed and worry, always on the look-out; the beaver works relentlessly; the bird pecks while keeping watch for the enemy, forced to both feed itself and protect itself. But when you're near a cow, she contemplates you briefly without seeing you, and then goes back to her grazing as if to say: I'm working, be on your way. Her weary gaze at human activities is in fact one of deprecation: these people have nothing else to do but walk around or take a train instead of grazing, grazing and making milk. Just knowing that in Denmark seasoned cellists come to entertain these ladies of the cowshed, playing concertos for them, fills me with joy: cows are great lovers of soothing music, which is a sign of their good taste. The cello, alongside the horn, is perhaps the instrument that is best suited to the mineral nature of high mountains. And the happy mathematics of Bach is the music that is closest to the chaotic geometry of peaks.

What could be more moving during summer than the season's joyous murmurs – the mocking whistle of woodchucks, the chirping of jackdaws, and the sharp notes of bells hanging from the collars of cows? These fairies of the sloping kingdom are the true sentinels of the mountain. Sometimes, in their mooing, I hear something like a call for help: 'Free me! I'm a cheerful young girl who has been trapped in this body by the spells of a sorcerer.' Every cow seems to keep something of her former condition in the softness of her eyes, the liveliness of her neck, her hint of a smile, and above all in her thin legs, sheathed in white – you'd almost expect her to begin dancing a waltz or a salsa. With their cheerful moods, certain heifers display the traits of adolescence: brazenness, casual insolence, reluctance to work, and the tendency to pout and rebel by running far away from the herd, until a border collie or an Australian shepherd brings them back. If my hypothesis is right, these young people still retain traces of their former existence. They're struck by bouts of playfulness and madness that differentiate them from the more serious older cows, held to the ground by the weight of their anatomy. The younger ones move about awkwardly; you'd swear they'd confused their hooves with high-heeled shoes. They're curious about everything: books left on a bench or a gate, whose pages they devour regardless of the title or the publisher; peelings of potatoes or cabbage; four-by-fours that pass by on trails; people out for a hike; diners at high-altitude cafés whose plates they, like goats, love to smell. A young cow is mischievous: she loves to flirt, getting lost in tête-à-têtes with a companion whose neck she sniffs, whose snout she kisses, whom she follows everywhere. If you scratch the head of a heifer or a calf at that place where a little tuft of hair grows in the shape of a ridge, they rest their head against you, and long trickles of contentment drip from their pink nose onto your shirt. Tenderness and simplicity converge in these promontories of horns and leather.

In 1826, an extraordinary event took place: the giraffe given to the king of France, Charles X, by the pasha of Egypt, Mehmet Ali, arrived in Marseille. Her journey – on foot – to Paris in the spring of 1827, which would last six weeks, and was supervised by the naturalist Geoffroy Saint-Hilaire (to whom Balzac dedicated *Le Père Goriot*), would take the form of a triumphal march. People came running from everywhere to see her, to admire her: they were utterly astonished, and until her death in 1845, the giraffe, originally from the Sudan, would attract millions of visitors, and would be the subject of many paintings and drawings. A small detail: in her journey to the capital, she was accompanied by three Egyptian cows – another offering of the viceroy – who nourished the giraffe in the mornings and the evenings, and who brought up the rear of the procession. I take great delight in this collaboration between species.

In 1981, in Jaisalmer, in Rajasthan, while I was sleeping on a straw mattress laid on the ground alongside a friend in a guest house in the upper part of the city, I was woken one morning by a bovid – a very young heifer – with eyes that had been made up. She had pushed open the multi-coloured curtain that served as a door, and was licking the tip of my nose with her warm, moist tongue. It was one of the sweetest awakenings of my life. At first I thought I was being attacked, but her mooing seemed to say: 'Get up, it's a pity to sleep so late when you should be out exploring the city!' My companion let out a cry of surprise, huddled beneath her sheet, and exclaimed: 'What kind of crazy country is this?' As a kind of welcome gift to the Rajput kingdom, the young cow dropped a large piece of dung in the middle of the room, and set off again in a dignified manner, shaking her tail to chase away the flies. The general manager assured us that it was a sign of luck: being chosen by a divine creature who leaves her excretions for you is a very good omen. He nonetheless began to wash our things, and offered me, as a parting gift, a kind of lucky charm: a fragment of the precious refuse in a little silver box. Since that day, I've had a strong affection for India and its cows.

A few years later, in Calcutta, in a far less elegant guest-house, I was given a dilapidated and windowless room with wobbly chairs, a bed with teetering legs, and a rocking chair with a hole through which my behind touched the floor. Starting from the first night, I was awakened by a large rat who slid under the door with difficulty and then went to join his friends in the bathroom, after a copious dinner in the kitchen. I informed the owner. He explained to me that it was impossible to lay traps or set out poisoned seeds because the rat was the vehicle of Ganesh, the god of prosperity, and was thereby sacred. He offered to lend me a cat so as to scare the creature. Around 11 p.m. he brought me an old one-eyed tomcat with a scratched coat full of bald spots, who gave me a threatening look and lay down, meowing, in the corner of the room. The rat always came by between midnight and 1 a.m., with a punctuality that Kant would have admired: the German philosopher left his house every morning at the same time to go on his walk and only ever deviated from his schedule twice – upon hearing the news of the storming of the Bastille, and on the publication of Rousseau's *Essay on Inequality*. The rat had barely had time to flatten himself out and cross beneath the door when the tomcat stood up and started to hiss. The surprised rat hesitated for a moment but refused to deviate from his path and bared his teeth. This had the desired effect. After a few customary meows, the tomcat climbed onto the bed and came toward me so I would protect him. The rodent kept on his way, barely quickening his pace, and giving us a look of contempt. The cat spent the rest of the night at my feet, snoring loudly and smelling bad. I thought about the Christmas dinner menu during the Paris Commune, when the capital, dying of hunger, hunted every animal it could: cat with a side of rats. I finally gave up all pretensions to regulating the animal traffic and got used to sleeping, for that entire week, with these small beings scampering about my feet.

Mountains, with their herds of bovines, thus bring me back to India. I like the Indian custom of putting makeup on mammals, often zebus with their oily humps and ample skin on their necks: people paint them red, adorn their horns with foliage, and mark their foreheads with sandalwood. Their dung, like toys left behind by children, marks out signs of presence that are best avoided. I don't mind this great civilization considering this animal as the universal Mother, Gao Mata, just like the ancient religions of Egypt, Greece and Rome, or certain pastoral cultures of Africa; even if this adulation, in the Indian subcontinent, gives rise to all sorts of political manipulation, and whips up crowds to riot. The prohibition on slaughtering these animals provides an occasion for all sorts of conflicts between Hindus and Muslims. A range of imported products, including tallow, lard, and vegetable oil, is an object of suspicion that can lead to an insurrection – such is the fear of impurity or sacrilege.

The cow continues to structure life in India in the same way as rice and the monsoon. Since the time of the Vedas, she has been the sacred animal, the universal and nourishing mother that was killed from time to time to share her meat so as to honour a guest. Historically, she passed from the Vedic stage (as an animal to be honoured and sacrificed) to the Hindu stage (as a revered animal whose killing constituted a crime), when Brahmins adopted a vegetarian diet based on the idea of non-violence (Ahimsa) from Jainism and Buddhism. The cow, who was assisted in this elevation of her status by the equally sacred character of the bull, himself the vehicle of Siva, was consequently associated with India, linking mother with fatherland. The buffalo, meanwhile, with his black skin, embodies untouchability, and can be eaten by beings who are themselves impure. Everything about the cow is blessed, including her urine, which is used in Ayurvedic medicine, and her dung, which is used to make fuel patties, ointments that are turned into dye for young women, and even a food that certain Brahmins absorb in a dried state to protect themselves from impurities. Ghee, the clarified butter with a slightly rancid odour made from cow milk, is used to anoint statues of divinities.

Certain holy cities of the subcontinent, such as Varanasi or Rishikesh, are above all cities of the cow, which is omnipresent and moos at will. From the train station to the *ghats* that descend toward the Ganges, she is there, in the narrowest of alleys, behind the humblest of shacks, alone or in groups, emaciated, stretched out in the middle of the road, blocking cars, getting up with an infinite slowness, empress of indifference, sleeping on sidewalks, and lending enormous cities the feel of country towns. Nowhere does this milk-filled and slightly ungainly wineskin appear happier with her lot, unconcerned with worldly affairs. Nowhere is the privilege of being born a cow brought to light like in the subcontinent. Her rumination leads men to chew over the truths of scripture; the gentleness of her eyes calls forth compassion and benevolence. When all is said and done, the cow, who always seems to be intensely meditating on the condition of living beings, is the philosophical animal par excellence. With her slow, doe-eyed pondering, she unites the generosity of a mother with the wonder of a sage. All the great gods of Hinduism have been linked to the cow: Krishna, the divine herdsman, was accompanied by dapper young cows during his stay on earth, and even Mahatma Gandhi wrote moving pages about this peaceful mammal, describing her as 'a poem of pity', a link of 'brotherhood between man and beast', the representative of 'the helpless and weak in the world', the 'mother to one and all'.[1] Given all this, it's easy to understand why in India eating a cow is seen as an act more terrible than cannibalism: it would be like eating your own mother, or even devouring the flesh of a god.

Do the cows of the Alps or the Pyrenees (breeds such as Abondance, Gasconne, Tarentaise), with their lovely white and mahogany dresses and their lyre-shaped horns, wish they could emigrate to India? They certainly wouldn't find the same profusion of pastures, but at least they'd have a secure retirement plan. India has invented a one-of-a-kind institution: the *goshala*, a retirement home for old or stray bovids. I've visited two of them, one in Varanasi, the other in Chennai. Financed by municipalities or munificent philanthropists, they accommodate old or sick animals – cows, oxen, bulls – to save them from the horrors of the slaughterhouse, the chance events of a nomadic life, or simply bad treatment. There they have green pastures, or at least an abundance of hay, after a life spent in traffic jams and crowded cities grazing on garbage or kilometres of old newspapers. In a loving and harmonious atmosphere, surrounded by walls painted with lovely frescoes, the knock-kneed and sometimes blind animals receive veterinary care and are venerated by the faithful, who bring them bundles of hay and sugarcane, and go so far as to kiss the ground on which they tread with a peculiar fervour. If I were a bovid, which might be the case in a future life, I would probably prefer European alpine pastures, but I'd opt for India in old age. It's not forbidden for benefactors to organize this kind of transfer, taking into account the climate and the linguistic and cultural shock. No other people and culture, aside from those of Madagascar perhaps, have swathed these animals in such an ambiance of legend and marvel. These bucolic paradises for the preservation of our horned grandmothers are deeply touching.

Whenever I ascend the inlays of a mountain pasture, I love being greeted by the bellowing of a cow who watches me pityingly as I try, at my age, to confront a summit instead of sitting in a café, sipping a lait grenadine or a milkshake.

CHAPTER 4

# The Mesmerizing Confederation

Here I am again in this land 'that God created to be horrible'
(Montesquieu). The admiration of mountains is an invention of
Protestantism. ... Switzerland: a wonderful reservoir of energy;
one has to go down how far? to find abandon and grace,
laziness and voluptuousness again, without which neither art
nor wine is possible. If of the tree the mountains make a fir,
you can imagine what they can do with a man. Aesthetics and
ethics of conifers.

ANDRÉ GIDE[1]

What is Switzerland? A mountain range that became a
nation at the heart of Europe, a living conservatory of the
customs of yesteryear, a safe that is impregnable for foreign
armies. I lived there intermittently for four years, between
the ages of six and ten, in a sanatorium in Leysin (at 1,200
metres altitude) called Les Noisetiers, under the guidance
of a group of female doctors and devoted nurses. Along
with the other children, I followed a routine: I inhaled
sulphur vapours, took a daily nap, had my temperature
taken in the morning and evening, was given a weekly

check-up, had lung x-rays, and went on long sledge outings during winter. Four marvellous years. No invalid has ever been happier than I was, far from my parents and from urban ugliness. I love dormitories, public lectures, and improvised theatre sketches. Illness is deeply instructive for those it doesn't kill: it separates those who contract it from those who don't, and as such is a noble distinction. Whenever one of our young classmates missed the evening roll call, we would be told that he had returned home; such removals always took place at night or at dawn, through the back door of the building. At Les Noisetiers they force-fed me: I was tubercular, rachitic, and so they stuffed me like a goose, per the abhorrent post-war norms that created generations of diabetics and obese people. They also made me forget my German by smacking me every time I spoke it: whenever I answered a question in the language of the Teutons, I would get a *calotte* (an old word for 'slap' that my mother used to use) and be prohibited from speaking. I came across the same intransigence once again when I was at the Sorbonne, where my teacher, Vladimir Jankélévitch, forbade his students from citing any twentieth-century German philosophers, all guilty, in his eyes, of having participated in the massacre. Fifty years later, I would learn that most of my classmates were Jewish children who were hidden behind pseudonyms. Some of them, being orphans, later made their way to Israel, where they were welcomed in accordance with the *Aliyah*. The trauma from the war was still fresh, and the hatred of the 'Krauts' persisted. I would have another experience of a sanatorium, this one maintained by the *Mutuelle des étudiants de France* health insurance provider, in Combloux at the beginning of the 1970s, to recover from hepatitis. I again had magnificent mountain surroundings, as I was facing the dome of Mont Blanc and the nearby Aiguilles Vertes. In Combloux I got to know several of the other convalescents, including a former combatant in the Algerian National Liberation Front (FLN), who was a little older than me and had never recovered from having participated, when he was very young, in the 1957 Melouza Massacre, during which the FLN killed the 374 inhabitants of this village in Kabylia, on the grounds that they were supporting the rival independence movement, Messali Hadj's *Mouvement national algérien*. Killing French people was perfectly acceptable, but shooting his own compatriots had made him sick, and he never recovered. He would often shout during uncontrollable bouts of rage, and would have to be pacified by the attendants.

In the villages close to Leysin, we would still come across many people suffering from goitre, though there were even more in the nearby Valais. Iodine treatments were just beginning to put a halt to this illness of the thyroid. We referred to these people as pelicans because of their enormous crops, and they inspired in us as much fear as fascination, despite their small stature and seeming mental infirmity. People with goitre had been discussed by Victor Hugo, and above all by Balzac, in his *Country Doctor*. But it was the anarchist geographer Élisée Reclus, who knew the Alps and Pyrenees very well, who went furthest in deprecating 'those hideous masses of living flesh'[2] who were fed swill with a spoon and who drooled on their tattered clothes.

I love Switzerland in the way one loves an imaginary fatherland that cannot be denigrated; I love it blindly, and I love it far more than Austria, which is too Germanic for me. From wherever you're standing in Switzerland, you can see at least one snowy peak, like an ivory figurine on the horizon. As soon as I cross the border, by way of the Jura or the Haute-Savoie, I have the absurd sense that I'm entering another world, one that is at once close to yet different from my own world, where the white cross on a red background says to me: here, you can't be reached by ordinary life. As with every love, this one is partial and infantile. The first thing I do after crossing the border, no matter what time it is, is to drink a hot chocolate. This is a rite of admission based on joyous recollections, in which I ingest, in little sips, a pure Swissness that bestows upon me an adoption certificate as it flows into my throat. I love the chaos of languages that you hear in everyday conversations in Switzerland, this mixture of dialects where Romansh, Italian, Vaudois French, and the different forms of *Schwiizerdütsch* – one for every mountain valley, spoken in the north and the east of the Confederation – all converge. I also love the rack-and-pinion trains, such as the one on the Jungfrau that climbs to 3,450 metres; the folkloric costumes that are dug out on every holiday; the Alphorns whose deep voices give me goose bumps; the singsong accent with its alternating speeds; even worse, I love the custom of yodelling, which brings me to tears (one of the best German yodellers today is a Japanese man named Takeo Ishii). This form of singing, which was originally used to call cattle from one valley to another, has become a musical genre in its own right, one that requires a particularly agile glottis. And I won't even speak of Swiss watches – veritable masterpieces of horology whose function is to wipe away the crime of passing time by creating items that last forever. I collect them in moderation – their exorbitant price prohibits me from acquiring too many of them. Each purchase is the fruit of a great deal of reflection. Switzerland, with its tiny share of exoticism that I find so attractive, is the quintessence of my passion for mountains: when I'm there, it's as though an invisible wall protects me from reality, even making the Confederation itself less real. (Haute-Savoie, that very Swiss part of France, is my second home.) Switzerland has responded to the enormity of its mountains with small-scale creations: miniature trains, funiculars, cable cars, and chalets. The country makes you feel like a child confronting an immensity that is all around. Its charm is that of an immaculately constructed model that reproduces reality to the nearest millimetre.

In the commune of Les Rousses in the Jura, there is an establishment called L'Arbezie, at once a hotel, a restaurant, and a café, that straddles the French–Swiss border, and is a perfect embodiment of my geographical fantasy: its kitchen is Gallic, while its salon is Helvetian. You can have an aperitif on the French side, and a coffee on the Swiss side. You move from one country to the other as you climb the staircase. As you lie in your hotel bed, your head is in France and your feet are in Switzerland: it is as though your body were separated from its extremities, requiring you to show your passport before touching your knees or toes. This imaginary demarcation delights me. Crossing borders becomes a game, turning me into a man from nowhere. During the war, the owner helped Jews and English pilots across the border: the German authorities only had access to the French section, but the staircase, starting from the seventh step, was in Switzerland. The Vichy regime walled off the French side. During the negotiations of the Évian Accords, the French and Algerian diplomats found themselves on either side of this imaginary line. L'Arbezie has become a little principality, with its own flag and its own administration.

I'm aware of all the accusations that are levelled at the Helvetic Confederation: it launders the money of dictators and criminals in its banks, it gives encouragement to tax exiles, it adheres to a neutrality that is all too convenient, it is a brain-dead democracy that has turned hypocrisy into an art form. Yet many authors, such as Voltaire, Rousseau, and Benjamin Constant, have celebrated it as a haven of freedom. For them, it was a land of refuge, just as it was right up to 1945 for certain persecuted Jews. Rousseau considered Switzerland to be a new Sparta, exempt from the corruption of cities and civilization – a union of freedom and simplicity, and the very example of primitive communism. He even predicted the birth of the sanatorium when he prescribed 'bathing in healthy and regenerative air'.[3] The only discordant voice in this concert of praise is that of André Gide, lover of the sun and of nudity among children (for which, today, he'd be tried in a court of law), who excoriated the unity of hygiene and puritanism in the Swiss.

There is one nineteenth-century writer, by contrast, who puts forth an unexpected portrayal of this nation: I'm speaking of Alphonse Daudet, and his book *Tartarin on the Alps*. In this picaresque novel about the ridiculousness of tourism, Daudet develops an incredible thesis: Switzerland does not exist. It is nothing more than a false décor, a theatrical machine set up by a crafty tourist board to entertain the English, Americans, and – as we'd say today – Asians, above all Japanese. Tartarin, who has been duly forewarned of this deception, refuses to let himself be tricked; even when he climbs the Jungfrau, pushed and pulled up the slopes by his guides, he is convinced that the boulders are nothing more than cardboard cut-outs, and the snow refrigerated water that has been sprayed by bellows.

'Switzerland at the present time, *vé!* Monsieur Tartarin, is nothing more than an immense Kursaal, which is open from June till September – a panoramic casino, to which people crowd for amusement, from all parts of the world; and which a tremendously wealthy company possessed of thousands of millions, which has its head-quarters in Geneva, has *exploited*. Money is necessary, you may depend, to farm, harrow, and top-dress all this land, its lakes, forests, mountains, and waterfalls, to keep up a staff of *employés*, of supernumeraries, and to build upon all high places monster hotels with gas, telegraphs, and telephones all laid on. [...] When you penetrate a little farther into the country, you will not find a corner which is not fixed up and machined like the floor beneath the stage in the Opera: waterfalls lighted up, turnstiles at the entrances of glaciers, and, for ascents of mountains, railways – either hydraulic or funicular',[4] as a certain Gonzague Bompard, a native of Tarascon in southern France just like Tartarin, explains to our hero. When Tartarin points out the existence of crevasses, the man replies that at the bottom of each crevasse there is 'a porter – a *chasseur* – somebody who is able to assist you up again, who will brush your clothes, shake off the snow, and respectfully inquire whether "Monsieur has any luggage?"'[5]

In this story, everything in Switzerland is fictional, or rather fake, like in the Jim Carrey movie *The Truman Show*: even the moon, 'blue, and liquid', is a prop, and even the light is the light of a cinemascope, reflected by artificial glaciers. The shepherds on the mountains, the herdsmen, the cheesemakers, the peasant women with their traditional hats and costumes, the well-tended pastures, the docile herds with their heavy bells – all actors paid by the Company. Switzerland? It's nothing but cardboard cut-outs, Las Vegas *avant la lettre*, or, if one prefers, an enormous Potemkin village: the intoxicating power of the false. Accidents in the mountains, guides who disappear with their clients – these are so many parodies of news stories designed to kindle interest: the guides in question travel abroad for just enough time to be forgotten, and then come back. The Helvetians are not a people but a theatrical troupe that is handsomely rewarded to entertain foreigners. It's all just a tall tale.

This little-known novel by Alphonse Daudet seems to me, in fact, to be quite accurate. With dated words, he expresses what I feel when I go to Switzerland: this sense of arriving in the world's backstage, in all the splendour of its artifice. Or rather, of its mixture of the false and the mythical. Knowing that there is at least one country that is a simulacrum, a scaffolding of appearances, reassures me. When I learned that an entire network of secret tunnels exists inside the Confederation's mountains, fortified bunkers where citizens can take refuge in the event of a nuclear war, I felt as though my intuitions had been confirmed. Switzerland is an underground novel. If it remains a waking dream for me, it's because when I go there, I return to the country of my childhood, one that is no less fanciful, and no less lost. It is the geographical illusion I need in order to tolerate France. There are cultures that are vital for their excess of reality, such as the United States; there are others that are just as vital for their avoidance or refusal of reality, where even death seems like playacting. I know this is a crazy vision, but it is one that allows me to attain a lightness of spirit as soon as I've crossed the Swiss border: there, I exist in an enchanted parenthesis, in the temporary suspension of all critical thought. If, as the Gnostics say, an evil demiurge has engendered a universe of misery and abomination, perhaps he forgot about this little canton at the heart of Europe. This is the naivety that I freely accept. Switzerland is the indispensable fiction that allows me to escape from history.

CHAPTER 5

# The Show-Offs and the Yokels

I hate mountains. They always seem like they're lecturing us.

PIERRE JEAN JOUVE

Today's infatuation with altitude is the contemporary version of an old dilemma in the history of travel: the opposition between the English aristocrat of the early nineteenth century who undertakes his grand tour of Europe, and the tourist of the twentieth who consumes countries the way others consume food from a menu. The term 'tourism' appeared in 1811 in England, and at the time it was imbued with nobility: as the contrary of 'travel', a variant of 'travail' that refers to the arduous utilitarian work of sailors and journeymen, 'tourism' connoted the Grand Tour, the circular voyage, a recreational activity to train and amuse the children of the upper classes. Tourism initially referred to the ostentatious expeditions of an idle elite who subsisted on their annuities; they benefited from the invention of the railroad, steamboats, and macadam, which allowed them to move about with great speed.

A reversal took place in the middle of the nineteenth century, when the bourgeoisie – that despicable class that was obsessed by calculation and profit – decided that they should go out and see the world. This was the beginning of a divorce that continues to this day. In *La Famille Fenouillard*, for example, which was the first French comic strip,[1] the eponymous family leave Normandy to travel as far afield as the North Pole and Japan. A bonnet maker who has grown rich, alongside his wife and their two simple daughters, Cunégonde and Artémise, unwillingly embark on a journey from Le Havre to America. This is the beginning of a whirlwind tour that carries them from New York to the Bering Strait, from the Sioux of the Great Plains to the Papuans of New Guinea. At each point in the journey, the awkwardness and stupidity of the French family is highlighted by the strangeness of the customs of those they encounter. We find a similar bourgeois satire in Eugène Marin Labiche's *Le Voyage de Monsieur Perrichon dans les Alpes* (1860). But the playwright goes beyond mockery: he writes a powerful allegory of ungratefulness in a mountain setting. Having thrown his daughter in a ditch, Monsieur Perrichon refuses to forgive her suitor for saving her. 'An imbecile is incapable of putting up for very long with the crushing burden known as gratitude.'

And so it is now the turn of the penpusher, the merchant, to go out and wander the world's vast spaces. The elite proclaims the end of tourism, for there can be no question of sharing its splendid migrations with shopkeepers who have been taken with wanderlust. It's too late: the most beautiful places have now been sullied by the industrious plebs. To climb is to flee a crowd that nonetheless catches up to you at the summit. The 'happy few' proclaim it loudly and clearly: the greatness of 'firsts', whether in the Himalayas or the Andes, is over, and the audience who followed them so closely has disappeared. Great exploits, with all their drama, no longer make the headlines. All the climbing routes are now equipped: the need for protection has clipped the wings of the pioneers. A semantic revolution has taken place: now, the term 'tourist' refers to anyone who joins the herd in its ceaseless motion. A word that once connoted the refined journeys of the few is now used to indicate the mass movement of the majority. This divide deepened in France in 1936, when the *Front populaire* granted the right to vacations to the entire population – the right, that is, to leisure, to picnics, to the sea, to the countryside. The mountains were a different matter: they benefited from a delay of sorts, given that the great climbers of the people and the democratization of snow appeared only in the 1950s and 1960s. What is a tourist? It's someone else – it's never us. Anyone who seeks to distinguish himself from the masses must curse the camper, the holidaymaker, the vacationer who diminish the quality of travel and sully immaculate summits with their mere presence. No gesture is more proper to tourism than the act of denouncing tourism. No less than the sea, mountains fit within romantic categories that oppose the aristocracy to the hordes, the authentic to the corrupt. The gladiators, armed with their karabiners, harnesses, and ice axes, look down on the people from Paris and Marseilles who go out with their backpacks to confront steep climbs and end up stumbling about awkwardly. They even invent derogatory terms for them: in Chamonix, vacationers are referred to as 'monchus' (a reference to the luxury restaurant of that name), while in the southern Alps, they're simply called 'cockroaches'.

In 2014, my comrade Jean-Christophe Rufin, a certified climber whom I met many years ago in Sudan, and who lives part of the year in the Haute-Savoie, said to me, as he watched masses of visitors climb the mountain paths:

'There go *les Bidochon*.'[2] I found the expression excellent and immediately applied it to myself. I lay claim to it with pride – at the time, I was setting out with my daughter for a walk around Mont Blanc, a *bambée* as they say in the Savoy region, in other words a little trot. Above 1,500 metres, you often encounter a very different type of person: the show-off of verticality. Whether they're men or women, they look down on you, immediately regarding you as a pampered and bumbling city dweller. They pass you on the walls with annoyance, for they don't like having you around – you slow them down. They are the enlightened ones who speak a secret language, full of codes and signs. They've crossed to the other side, having mastered a domain that the masses regard with apprehension. Don't misunderstand me: I have the greatest respect for climbers, and I share the opinion of Lionel Terray, who observes that many young climbers missed their calling as warriors or soldiers, pirates or corsairs. Climbing is a passion of sublimation in that it diverts aggression toward athletic challenges. It manifests a sadism of domination, as Gaston Bachelard says. But the recklessness, grace, and courage of climbers and guides does nothing to diminish our humble pleasure in reaching summits at our own pace. Mountains are big enough to host all sorts of families, including tenacious amateurs such as myself. We used to think of peasants as bumpkins, but by way of a strange inversion, today it is the strolling city dweller who has become the resident yokel, held in disdain by those who are 'pure'. These latter put their hands in their pockets and whistle, as I've seen children at Saint-Véran do to mock the simpletons (this is what they call us) who get stuck as they slowly scale walls. Pros recognize each other through gestures of complicity: the wall is his friend, his living room, his bedroom; he caresses it like an old throw, takes stock of it in a single glance, climbs it as easily as most people take the metro. The tourist can disguise himself as a Sherpa all he wants – he'll never stop being a hick.

For a long time we distinguished people of the plains, who are seen as more concerned with material reality, from mountain dwellers, who are regarded as idealists because they're closer to the sky. But in fact we're all prey to our worldly passions: the moment we think we escape human pettiness, we reproduce it. Mountains aren't open to everyone: there's a division that takes place according to age and ability. In our time, we find different activities super-imposed on the same mountains, a little like a millefeuille, and each of these activities seeks to have its rightful place. Amateurs puff and pant right beside specialists who engage in a fierce competition of show-offs flaunting their bravery, peacocks spreading their tails on summits, devotees with their phallic ice axes. The love of nature degenerates into a cult of accomplishments, a mad counting and collecting of summits. The Catalan 'ultraterrestrial' Kilian Jornet, with his extraordinary abilities, is symptomatic of this: he completed the return trip from the Church of Chamonix to the summit of Mont Blanc in four hours, fifty-seven minutes, and seventy-four seconds. Who can top that? He has broken several other records: the ascent of the Matterhorn from the Italian ski resort Breuil-Cervinia; that of Aconcagua in Latin America (6,962 metres); and finally that of Everest, which he climbed in thirty-eight hours starting from a monastery at 5,100 metres, without oxygen, fixed ropes, or a Sherpa. He followed these performances with a belated expression of remorse for his expansive carbon footprint. He is a veritable object of worship: it seems that people slept in front of his door when he was living in Chamonix so as to soak in his power. He has an unparalleled lung capacity, and his resting heart rate is forty beats per minute. Another example is Reinhold

Messner, the Italo-Austrian, an exceptional athlete who was the first person to climb all fourteen summits of more than 8,000 metres in elevation, and one of the first to reach the highest points of all seven continents. Not to mention Nirmal Purja, veteran of the British special forces, who in 2019 climbed fourteen 8,000-metre summits in six months and six days! It's the one-upmanship of those who seek to climb the highest and fastest, leaving in their wake those onlookers who can do nothing more than marvel at their performances. The English writers John Ruskin and D. H. Lawrence foresaw this, poking fun at the romantic frenzy of those who hoist themselves up to the top of a pillar like stylites, or who swagger about on mountain ridges, believing themselves to be masters of the earth, exposing their biceps and their courage for all to see. Rivalries are fierce among the initiated. In the best cases, it all takes the form of a game, a competition. Samivel, peerless illustrator and storyteller, also made fun, in the post-war years, of those haughty climbers who stood aloof from the crowd, evoking 'the tragic gaze of the hero who is turned toward his destiny'. Today, things are slightly different, in that the hero appears on television news programmes, climbing onto the stage beneath the gaze of the cameras, displaying the brands that sponsor him. Mountains lend themselves to posturing: just as there are old sea dogs, there are old mountain dogs as well.

I understand the intoxication of this kind of performance, the movements of these uncommon beings that are almost like those of a pendulum, swinging from spectacular acts to remorse, followed by a declaration of ecological faith: it doesn't do any harm. It's like a seducer who settles down at the end of his life and becomes an ascetic. We're in the realm of the Augustinian *felix culpa* or 'happy fault': the just person is not the innocent who has never made a mistake, but the sinner who repents.

First you step onto the podium to dazzle the audience, and then you promise never to do it again, to protect the mountain from any and all contamination. The public confession prolongs the entry in the *Guinness Book of Records*. Everyone collects peaks and mountain faces like a Soviet marshal collects medals on his chest. They flee from the mediocre world of men, but still submit to the illness of contemporary humanity: the spirit of calculation. I admire these superhuman beings, both men and women (among them Catherine Destivelle, who has now retired from extreme sports, and Stéphanie Bodet), who blow us away with their boldness and their skill; I look at them in the same way an earthworm looks at the stars. But their superiority in no way diminishes the pleasure I take in mountain hikes. Alexandre Dumas, speaking of Jacques Balmat, hunter of chamois and crystals and the first man to vanquish Mont Blanc in 1786, writes that, when Balmat arrived at the summit of this mountain, he cried: 'I'm the king of Mont Blanc', 'I'm the statue on this immense pedestal.'[3] At the time, his cry of pride was understandable: taming mountains as though they were so many trophies just lying about meant overcoming ancestral terror, and glorifying oneself for having trampled these titans underfoot. Today, it's the obsession with the 'ever more' that wins out: ever higher, ever further, ever faster. The career of a climber follows a standardized hierarchy: first the Alps, then the Urals and the Andes, and finally the crowning moment of the Himalayas – it's like an accumulation of plunder. Mountains, which are supposed to heal us from human emotions, exacerbate them, turning into the stakes of a hierarchy that can never be disarmed. Even *les Bidochon* stare stonily at one another, submitting each other to the same forms of exclusion as those to which their superiors submit them. The same fever for novelty inspires the jousting of these little roosters.

As such, the love of peaks follows a double movement: their democratization, on the one hand, is counterbalanced by an elitism, indeed a hyper-elitism, on the other. The elegant adventure of those few wealthy bourgeois who founded the *Club alpin français* at the beginning of the twentieth century[4] gives way to hikers who invade paths and ski stations. In his *Histoire d'une montagne* (1880), Élisée Reclus had already written of the civilized man who, at altitude, is caught between two passions, that of the climber and that of the walker. Those who walk as opposed to those who ascend; infantrymen versus warlords – these latter are subdivided into rock climbers and 'glacierists'. To the tightrope walkers of the void goes excellence; to those who shuffle along goes condescension. Other activities would be added later, such as trail running or mountain biking, the consequence of which is congestion on high-altitude footpaths. The walker is thereby joined on narrow trails by runners squeezed into fluorescent clothing, who come up behind him unexpectedly, with tubes in their mouths that they suck on continuously. Then there are the helmeted cyclists who pass by like a shot, almost colliding with him as they do so. All that's missing are scooters and four wheelers! The plebs grumble and step aside, slightly jealous of these sweaty and smelly athletes who climb and descend without even looking around, focused as they are on their imaginary exploits. They leave you in their dust and curse what, to them, is your vagrant appearance. They aim to be light as air, and are indifferent to the grade of the slope and the stones that block their way. Trail running is an example of the democratization of excess: its practitioners take pride in dominating the forces of gravity, in quickly crossing distances that mere mortals take hours to cover. At the Ultra-Trail du Mont Blanc, a race that takes place at the end of summer in Chamonix, an entire coterie of trotting experts and galloping big shots attacks the slopes. The hyper-individualism of the competition blends seamlessly into the gregariousness of speed. As you watch, you're tempted to ask them: aren't you suffering? From tendinitis, plantar fasciitis, torn arches? They look like Sherpas on cocaine. Regardless of their age, they hurl themselves at the trails, at the risk of grinding down their joints, destroying their vertebrae, or having a heart attack. And they do this in spite of their white hair, their knock knees, their flabby bellies: there's no other race that arouses the spirit of antagonism more powerfully than this one, especially among the younger of the senior citizens, who want above all else to stay in the game. The spectre of their old age and the inertia that comes with it gives them wings. The Ultra-Trail is their shock therapy: a maniacal fury and an addiction to wilful suffering takes hold of them, all beneath the supervision of well-paid sponsors – for the Ultra-Trail du Mont Blanc is above all a lucrative business.

There are many schools of mountaineering: moral rigour (Philippe Claudel[5]), the fraternity of the climbing party (Roger Frison-Roche), extreme adventure (Lionel Terray, Walter Bonatti, Anselme Baud), bold anarchy (Reinhold Messner), nuptial embrace with the void (Stéphanie Bodet), quasi-mystical asceticism (Erri De Luca), committed dandyism (Sylvain Tesson). You can love mountains without being tormented by a desire for heroism, without being obsessed by constantly reaching new heights or blazing new trails. Groups of climbers are no longer driven by patriotic or nationalistic ideals – today, the important thing is the personality of the climber. He undergoes ordeals worthy of the damned, pushes the limits of human endurance, and evokes – for the common mortal that I am – either a colossus or a crackpot. There are several periods in the literature of mountains: a period of exploration that took place between the two world wars; a post-1945 patriotic period; a Jansenist period, with its great discoverers. Today this literature is marked by a dominant individualism, a display of great performances wrapped up in the discourse of personal development and an ecology-laced neo-Buddhism. There's one thing I share with all these exceptional beings, if on a much smaller scale: fervour.

Even though we're all climbers, it's tempting to place us on one side or the other of an impossible alternative: tourists or purists. But a mountain is vast enough to accommodate all those who love it; it is a wicked yet generous stepmother who sometimes kills a few of her children while enchanting the others. There are those who want to dominate its rock faces, and those who climb to feel more intensely, to stand awestruck before its majesty. I belong to this latter group. I bow before the highest peaks without lamenting the fact that I can't climb them. I prefer the wisdom of the possible to the morality of achievement. For me, to climb is first and foremost to pray – to enter into a relationship with higher powers. I pray above all that my body will be up to the task, that it won't give out while I'm climbing. I understand the wills of those proud beings who confront that which is vaster than them; indeed, this is the very desire that defines the magnificent madness of youth. But sometimes you have to forgo the highest mountain ranges to find challenges that suit you. I have a great deal of love for the passage in Lionel Terray's book *Les Conquérants de l'inutile* in which this exceptional athlete describes his amazement when one of his clients – a Swiss German who has faultlessly climbed to the summit of the 3,478-metre Grépon (in the Mont Blanc range) in three hours – declines his guide's suggestion that they proceed to the south crest of the Aiguille du Fou so as to finish their exploit with one final crazy romp: 'Oh!

No, monsieur Terray, I'm not at all interested in ideas of that sort. I've never climbed as fast as that before, and I found it great fun, but that's enough for one day. What I like about mountaineering is being in touch with nature and looking at the scenery. Anyway, the weather's perfect, and since you're engaged for the day we'll just stay here until noon.'[6] This man was a philosopher who preferred peaceful celebration to frenetic speed.

It's strange to observe the extent to which climbs of 8,000 metres or more aroused both bitterness and sadness in the lives of certain great climbers. In his autobiography, Reinhold Messner, the Italo-Austrian who climbed the highest mountains on the globe as though he were collecting summits, alternates between telling the story of his great exploits and settling his scores with the German Alpine Club, who never stopped maligning him for the death of his brother on the descent of the Nanga Parbat (the highest summit in Pakistan, at 8,129 metres). It's as though the greatest enemy of climbers were other climbers. Walter Bonatti, tired of the jealousy and mudslinging of his colleagues, left the entire scene behind to focus on 'the exaltation of struggling in solitude'.[7] He himself had been betrayed by two climbing partners on the K2 in 1954, left to his fate in a bivouac at 8,100 metres, which could have proved fatal (he would settle the score forty years later in two books that showed his anger hadn't diminished in the slightest). These obsessed climbers inspire us, and rightly so, but they act in a way that is entirely human. And when they have success in a collective undertaking, such as Maurice Herzog on the Annapurna in 1950, alongside Louis Lachenal, Gaston Rebuffat, and Lionel Terray, mere Earth dwellers ceaselessly belittle them, going so far as to accuse them of lying. Maurice Herzog, who had his fingers and feet amputated – he gave a haunting depiction of the operation in his book – was canonized for his martyrdom, elevated to the rank of national hero at the expense of Louis Lachenal, who followed him to the summit purely out of friendship. But he was later revealed to be an egotistical tyrant, if we are to believe his daughter Félicité, who depicted him, in a beautiful and cruel novel, as a vain and lecherous patriarch, going so far as to accuse him of incest.[8]

Which raises an ancillary question. Today, there's no shortage of books in which children pillory their fathers and mothers: people talking about how much they hate their family is all the rage. Battered and abused children drag their progenitors before the court of public opinion, demanding some sort of vengeance. Should they settle their scores with their parents while they're still alive, or wait until they're dead (which I did with my own father)? It's a matter of personal ethics, and it will be interesting to see if the children of these very authors will in turn submit them to the same questioning, so as to avenge their grandfather or grandmother.

In the case of Maurice Herzog, who has since been exonerated from all suspicion of duplicity where the veracity of his story is concerned, it's impossible not to think of Hegel's famous dictum: 'No man is a hero to his valet, not because the former is no hero, but because the latter is a valet.' But these princes of altitude leave themselves wide open to attack in their envy of one another – the same thing happens in every profession. They hold long-lasting grudges, seeking to defend their reputations at all costs. The fact that they inhabit great heights doesn't shield them from ordinary rivalries. And once they've run their race, the following generations cross swords with them. The battle of egos rages on: we believe we've vanquished our worst failings, but in fact we bring them along with us to the summit. Why should things be any different? Let us admire great acts while forgetting the pettiness of the actors.

CHAPTER 6

# Lived Experiences

It's the morning that instils belief. You must always start at
dawn when you walk, to accompany the awakening day.

FRÉDÉRIC GROS, *A PHILOSOPHY OF WALKING*[1]

At the foot of the Dôme des Écrins, after a long succession
of seracs as formidable as a row of canine teeth, we arrive
at a wall of ice at 4,000 metres that you have to climb.
That morning – 15 August, 9:30 – we'd been up since
three. We form a queue under the patient command of our
guides. It's already too warm, barely zero degrees Celsius,
meaning there's a threat of thawing. An old Englishman,
wearing glasses (he's only old in my eyes – he can't be more
than fifty-five), accompanied by his daughter, decides to
climb all alone, without asking for anyone's permission.
The ice glistens above him like fish scales on which you
might cut your hands. He's not going to let the 'Frenchies'
call the shots. He's completely seized by a narrow-minded
bravura, a rebellious flair – a Brexiteer before his time. His
daughter warns him – 'Daddy, be careful' – but he attacks

the ice with his axe, doing so with a bit too much vigour and tearing off an enormous block of ice that hurtles down the wall, almost killing those waiting patiently. The guides heap abuse on him, ordering him to come down and let the others go first. He returns in a pitiful state, where his daughter reprimands him sharply. He apologizes and sits down, overcome with emotion; I think I see tears in his eyes. Cries of 'Daddy' burst forth, but they're not signs of affection – they're more like knife blades. There's nothing worse for a parent than for his children to be ashamed of him. An hour later, he arrives at the summit, humiliated, having lost the respect of the person he wanted to impress. I'm sad for him and feel like consoling him. The kingdom of splendour has been transformed into one of dishonour.

A high mountain often constitutes a test. I recall a young and quite elegant Italian couple I once saw in a hut in the Briançonnais zone, constructed around 1940 by the *Club alpin français* (it looks like a beached boat at 2,800 metres, and smells of urine and lentils). Their relationship seems to be one of those that are founded on reciprocal narcissism, as though they form a little society of mutual admiration. They clash with the shaggy and unkempt climbers who form the majority of their group: they're wearing the very latest fabrics, outfits worthy of fashion week runways; they have million-dollar smiles and perfect hair; they're heading out to attack the peaks with the wolfish grins of winners. You can barely imagine them taking part in the cordial quibbling of climbing parties. At 2 p.m., the young man returns alone and distraught. He bashfully explains to the hut's caretaker that his fiancée is right behind him. When she arrives two hours later, completely dishevelled and having lost half of her equipment, all hell breaks loose. She's lost her superb appearance, but not her voice. As far as we can make out, he abandoned her on the glacier, exasperated by her slowness. He left her behind so he could go faster. A major mistake. She hurls insults at him, breaks down in tears, gathers her things, and heads back down alone toward the valley. He doesn't try to stop her. A monstrous thought comes to me: was he hoping she'd fall into a crevasse so he could get rid of her?

As you approach the col, your phone starts ringing out with notifications: your signal has returned, and with it come one message after another. You don't dare to look at them – your partners are all giving you dirty looks. Once you arrive, you turn on your phone with frozen fingers, but the signal is gone. You curse and swear that the next time, you're going to hold up the whole team to find out who's trying to reach you. When you finally read the texts, precariously holding onto a tiny grip, it's like a cold shower: advertisements, unknown numbers, and two pocket dials. The mobile phone is the instrument of modern 'Bovarysme': high expectations followed by unfathomable disappointment.

In the Valais in Switzerland, near Arolla, I'm climbing, all alone, toward a col that joins up with the Mountaineer's Route from Chamonix to Zermatt. The Matterhorn stands in the distance like an arched pyramid. There's a low hill overlooking the col, which I climb for the view. Not far below me, I see a large stone platform on which a man and a woman, both completely naked, present their bodies to the sun's rays. They're in the lotus position with their eyes closed, trying to connect with the cosmos. Unfortunately for me (given my voyeuristic tendencies), they're no spring chickens. And when they get up to stretch their legs, I see two bodies on the verge of collapse. Neither of them have buttocks. Their behinds have been blown by the wind and hang down in folds like old rags. I turn away and leave without making a sound. They climbed to 3,000 metres to search for a fountain of youth, a rejuvenation by way of ultraviolet rays. I come across them that evening at the Hotel Kurhaus, both very dignified, wearing the local costume; they're speaking to each other in *Schwiizerdütsch* and drinking a little Fendant, neat. As a mood-enhancing drug, alcohol is stronger than exposure to high altitudes. I watch them, vaguely embarrassed to share their secret. They believe – I believe it even more strongly – in the Helvetico-Protestant myth against which André Gide railed: that of regeneration by way of climbing. And suddenly I imagine everyone in the dining room secretly sitting naked on the rocks in the first light of dawn, as though they were a sect. A nightmare of good health, worthy of Polanski's *Rosemary's Baby*.

Anyone who climbs learns that he does not control his digestive tract. Should this lead us to feel dishonour or relief? Beyond 2,500 metres, your insides make their own rules, and woe to anyone who tries to disregard this. Because I'm quite familiar with this type of debacle – through an episode on the Trient glacier, when I was climbing with my daughter and a guide (they were kind enough to give me some space) – I know that in the high mountains, we're nothing but guts, scorched lungs, anxious heart, and upset stomach. The union of fear and altitude gives rise to accelerated discharges. It's the end of dignity. There's nothing you can do to stop these emergencies. The great adventurer and mountaineering champion Stéphanie Bodet recounts how, while in an acrobatic posture on the Grand Capucin (3,838 metres), she had to lower her pants to relieve a pressing need.[2] She notes that on El Capitan, the famous vertical rock formation in Yosemite National Park in the western United States, climbing teams must bring with them a 'poop tube', an airtight plastic tube for excrement, which they carry behind them, at the risk of dropping unique sprinkles on those who are climbing behind them. And certain cliffs, which are already terrifyingly difficult to climb, are covered in faeces, a little like the way Parisian sidewalks are sprinkled with dog droppings. The poetry of the mountains has its limits.

It's as though Narcissus had been put in his place. You make detailed preparations for your climb, you train for weeks, you consider every possible route, you check the forecast. When the day arrives, you and your companions begin the ascent like stubborn snails, in suffering and agony, loudly gasping for air. Several hours later, you finally reach the peak you've been aiming for. A surge of pride engulfs you. That evening, back at the hut, you tell the tale of your achievement with all the discretion that immodesty allows. The locals react by saying: oh yeah, it's a nice little stroll. A NICE STROLL! I paid for your leisurely little walk with sweat and blood – I thought I was going to die!

The night before a climb is one of almost silent enchantment. In the distance we hear the cracking of a glacier, the banging of falling rocks. The stars, dotting the sky like so many beauty marks, seem so close that we could touch them. We're charmed by the fact that all this power seems subservient to all this silence. The sea bellows, but mountains rumble. There, the hypnotic effect of waves striking the beach; here, the crackling of the ground as it breathes. All around us, peaks stand out like shadow puppets, and the jagged crests and escarpments are candlesticks that rise up like the glaive of a swordsman. Early in the morning our crampons grip the hard snow nicely. Seeing dawn's pink vapours disperse around the peaks is magical. For a brief period of time, the sky is an indigo blue. The crystals shimmer in a perfect radiance. The day sets our minds straight, restoring the strength that night took away. We advance in a union of terror and respect that anticipates the religious emotion of the summit: what is at stake is indeed a form of the sacred that confronts us with something up above. We tread on the ground of another planet, a space that already belongs to the cosmos. The ecstasy makes you shudder. The silence at 2,500 metres is a low-level din, a false peace to which we have to acclimatize our ears. The peace is deceptive: we gaze with awe upon rocky spines, upon impregnable fortresses that challenge us. The strips of lapies, limestone formations that have been dug out by run-offs, are a coarse skin that we caress carefully, fearing their sharp bumps. On the descent, there is always time to sniff the little flowers that persist here: glacier buttercups, forget-me-nots, gentians. And there is something enigmatic about the odour exuded at nightfall by rocks that have cooked all day in the sun – it is as though the mineral realm had taken on the powers of the vegetal realm.

There exist metal or beech 'blueberry combs', used in the harvest at the end of the summer. This name delights me. I imagine myself styling the hair of a bush so as to collect its berries and bring them home.

Friendship means, above all, a small circle of passionate companions. It's not simply about shared affinities or common projects, but an entire apparatus of recip-rocal temptations. It brings out unsuspected aptitudes in everyone. A friend breathes into you a boldness that you previously lacked, and as such, he expands you. He's not only a witness to a common past, but a force that pulls you along with him. The same goes for a couple: a spouse or a partner is a goad who pulls you by the hand. Two are stronger than one, especially when the two act as a little commando unit. I remember ascending the Bromo, in Java, in 1977, on the back of a mule with my friend Laurent Aublin (who at the time was a diplomatic advisor in the French embassy in Jakarta) and his wife Pascale. We had slept in a hut the previous night, and when the sun rose at 6 a.m., we arrived at an immense sea of sand. The effect was striking: an apocalyptic landscape with the silhouette of a knight in the distance. The crater of this fire-breather resembled a pastry cone, a sort of giant *cannelet* from which rose fumes smelling of sulphur. It was a magical moment. I returned in 2019 to discover that the sacred mountain had been completely commercialized: you have to stand in line to go up to its upper rings. Its spell had vanished. I've visited other volcanoes, both extinct and active: the most devious or dangerous of the latter is the Montagne Pelée (1,397 metres) in Martinique, which killed 30,000 people in 1902 and will awake one day with convulsions and tremors. The cutest of them was the Soufrière volcano (2,500 metres) in Réunion: in my memory, the path to it was strewn with miniature craters, natural cooking pots that bubbled and simmered – so many small, warm, and sputtering orifices that looked like molehills, and that made you want to clean them like the Little Prince on his asteroid. Most of the time, eruptions kill and devastate, like in Goma in western Congo, or La Palma in the Canaries. They also fascinate. When a volcano awakes, like in Iceland in 2021, opening up cracks and expelling a phantasmagoria of colours – streams of orange light on a background of black basalt – it's a global event, an occasion to celebrate. People come from all over to sing, dance, and play volleyball around it; newlyweds pose before flows of incandescent lava; people cook sausages or steaks on its burning rocks. The effervescent mountain becomes a friend for the people who celebrate its eruption while taking care to avoid its flames.

I'm ten years old, and I'm in Megève, skiing with my mother. We're staying in the Hôtel des Sapins, a little two-star establishment whose kitchen serves generous portions. We take the old Rochebrune ski lift, a metal perch shaped like an anchor to which is attached a double seat made of hazel wood that shakes you about, and that you descend from on opposite sides at the arrival. A few metres from the summit, feeling the tension both of the cable and of fear, I fall to the left, while my mother totters on the right. The whole mechanism stops, and I hurtle down the slope. This marks the beginning of an apprehension that will last years. The next day, we take the same lift and arrive almost to the end before we both fall. It's as though we're performing a little ballet in which one person's incompetence begets the other's uselessness. As though my mother had inoculated me with her weakness, or I had increased hers. She should have scolded me and forced me to try again until I succeeded. Instead, we were now debilitated, and took to climbing up on our skis rather than using the mechanical installations. This is how my childhood phobias got started. I'd like to go back a half century into the past so as to overcome this ridiculous obstacle with her. I gave up my grudges and anger toward my parents a long time ago; above all, I wish I could reconcile them by wresting them from that reciprocal demolition that was their marriage. Perhaps life after death is comprised of reconciliation rooms in which men and women, brothers and sisters, and couples who have been torn apart settle their accounts, embrace, cry, and ask for forgiveness.

In Switzerland once more, we hesitate while standing before a series of dizzying ladders, two almost vertical stretches to descend onto the glacier and make our way to the Dix mountain hut on the Zermatt-Chamonix Mountaineer's Route (the ladders have since been renovated). We have no ropes, and the slightest bit of vertigo, the smallest faux pas, would be fatal. I'm scared I'll get to a certain point and not be able to move, stuck against the bars like a huge butterfly pinned to the wall. Suddenly a hardy octogenarian arrives wearing leather pants and a feathered hat. He grabs hold of the first ladder's handrail and begins descending.

'Come on, youngsters, just do it!'

His cajoling doesn't work. We watch the plumes of his hat disappear and turn back.

Learning that it's minus 43 Celsius at the Aiguille du Midi on 8 April 2021 delights me more than all the figures of the stock market. This record cold is crazy – it's like having the North Pole in my own country. But in mid-September of the same year, the geometers discover that Mont Blanc has shrunk by 90 centimetres since the last reading in 2017. Consternation reigns in the valley of Chamonix. People keep watch over the colossus like a child whose slightest toothache or fever causes concern.

I remember the little train station at Villars-sur-Ollon, at 1,200 metres, in the canton of Vaud in Switzerland, invaded by a commando unit of goats who found nothing better to do than to climb aboard as soon as the funicular arrived and to await its departure. I can only imagine the dialogue between these law-breakers and the ticket inspector.

Here's a story of a cold shower. Sixteen years ago, I arrived in the early afternoon with a friend from Mauritius to the Agnel mountain hut, at 2,850 metres, after having visited the abandoned copper mines near Monte Viso. It's very hot, we're burned and dehydrated, and we drink several litres of water. A stranger comes up to me with a smile, and says: 'I really like what you do.' I take on the bewildered look of someone whose ego has just been stroked. He continues: 'But sometimes you make silly pronouncements.' He reminds me of a recent radio interview in which I said that if God really exists, he's either a bastard or a weakling. The stranger then embarks on a long diatribe on the freedom that the Creator bequeathed to humanity. I've stumbled upon an annoyed Christian who refutes every one of my arguments. I persist and, though he perseveres for a while, he finally gets up, furious. I'm just as furious at myself for not having been able to convince him. Since then, whenever I arrive at a hut, I prepare myself for an improbable theological discussion with some quarrelsome person. Even in these places that lend themselves so well to concord and fraternity, God still manages to divide people.

I'm an average lover: I love the piano and mountains, but I'll never be a pianist or a mountain dweller, just a dilettante. When I sit before the piano, I dream of enchanting arpeggios, frenzied boogies, and dizzying Charlestons, and I always come up against the same limits. Every cliff, every rock face, says to me: not for you. Why love what rejects you? Why persist in the more or less? Why not? If you had to be a professional at everything you have a taste for, you'd never try anything. I'm laborious at the piano, I'm stubborn and stoic on the slopes, but that doesn't mean I'm any less happy to try, to insist.

Nietzsche's house in Sils Maria is a must-see. Repainted in blue, white, and red, it looks like an advertisement in a real estate magazine. It was there, in 1881, that the idea of Zarathustra came to him, at '6,000 feet above the sea, and at a much higher altitude above all human affairs'[3] (6,000 feet will never be any higher than 2,000 metres). The inside of the house tells a different story, one of the heavy hand of the sister who literally sold her brother's work to national socialism. The master's bedroom is sparse: a rustic bed, a table, a chair, an old jug. In the photos, the philosopher with the proud Prussian moustache seems, with his hunched profile, to be disoriented. He's already an old man who has miraculously survived his mental illness thanks to the air in Engadin, where his sister has brought him. This is where he'll be resurrected, through the light, the beauty of the surroundings, the clarity of the hills. But the madness that will carry him away is looming. Everything in Engadin, he writes, is 'grand, still and bright'.[4] 'The ice is near, the solitude is immense – but how peacefully everything lies in the light! how freely you breathe! how much you feel to be *beneath* you! – Philosophy, as I have understood and lived it so far, is choosing to live in ice and high mountains.'[5] In a mean-spirited way, Theodor Adorno tells the story of how children threw gravel into Nietzsche's umbrella, so that a storm of stones fell upon his head as soon as he opened it. As for the famous boulder where he meditated after his long walks, and where he supposedly had the inspiration for the eternal return, it's nothing more than a stone beside a lake. Three French students who came upon it at the same time as us told us how disappointed they were. Nietzsche writes: 'the secret for harvesting from existence the greatest fruitfulness and the greatest enjoyment is – *to live dangerously*!'[6] The great English mountaineer Joe Simpson, quoting this passage, makes the following conclusion about it: 'He might have thought twice about that one if he had been handed a pair of ice tools and pushed in the general direction of Bridalveil Falls'[7] (a 188-metre waterfall in Yosemite National Park, California).

The birthplace of a great body of thought is revealing, and there is always the risk of dressing it up, ceding to the temptation of 'pathetic embellishments'. The pictures in the house in fact show a tired old man who took a little walk every day around Lake Silvaplana. To age is to forget how to walk – to 'unlearn' walking, as it were. The foot trembles with each hesitant step, and the slightest incline becomes a threat. You can discern someone's age from the way he climbs or descends a staircase. It's difficult to celebrate dance, climbing, the thought of open air, the thought that arises from wandering, and at the same time to be confronted with your own weak and weary body. The risk is that of philosophizing beyond yourself. The man who wanted to think like a soaring eagle and confront those with 'hard sit-and-wait flesh'[8] appears, in the photos, to be old and out of breath, on the verge of insanity. And I can't help perceiving, in a certain Nietzscheanism – that of the Overman, Zarathustra, the praise of the blond beast – a pompousness that dissolves in these photos, this evidence. In a chapter entitled 'On the Rabble', he has his prophet say: 'And like strong winds we want to live above them, neighbours to eagles, neighbours to snow, neighbours to the sun: thus live strong winds.'[9] But I think of Nietzsche's eagle as more of an anaemic cormorant or an old pigeon. It's the tragedy to which we are all susceptible – that of posturing. The body of work reinvents the person who created it after the fact; Nietzsche invented 'great health' as a way of overcoming one illness by way of another.

We don't always walk on a path of meditation: Nietzsche perfectly illustrates the chasm between rhetoric and reality. For he is the man of high plateaus, as Bachelard rightly said, and not of peaks. His ascension is above all imaginary: he transforms heaviness into lightness and 'makes abysses speak the language of summits'.[10] Nietzsche is the man who comes down from the medium-sized mountain to deliver his messages to his fellow men, the sheeplike crowd, to 'the last human being, who makes everything small'.[11] In his most elitist or dated aspects, he makes me think of the scene in Carol Reed's *The Third Man* in which Orson Welles, on the great Ferris wheel in the Prater amusement park in Vienna, explains that men seen from above are nothing but worthless ants. Nietzscheans tire me – they always overdo things. I revere Nietzsche's multi-faceted genius and I adore mountains. But I can easily see how the meeting of the two can predispose fragile minds to delusions of superiority. Didn't the totalitarianisms of the twentieth century – Nazism, fascism, communism – exalt high mountains as schools of patriotism and virility? In 1937, Hitler extolled the first conquerors of the north face of the Eiger (which resulted in several deaths); the German Alpine Club forbade Jews membership until 1945. In the USSR, the Abalakov brothers climbed the vertiginous Stalin Peak (7,495 metres) and the Lenin Peak to glorify the 'Father of Nations', who thanked them by handing them over to the purges of the Great Terror.[12] 'For the fatherland, for the mountain' was for a long time the motto of the *Club alpin français* and of the first Himalayan expeditions. Today it is no longer nations who confront summits: successes and injuries are now part of the private domain. But the snobbery of distinction is better than bellicose myths. Go visit Nietzsche's house in Sils Maria – it will cure you of your Nietzscheanism.

CHAPTER 7

# The Aesthetics of the Adventurer: Princes and Peasants

> Men fall off mountains because
> They have no business being there.
> That's why they go, that's why they die.
>
> SID MARTY, CANADIAN POET[1]

Our epoch has reunited us with our bodies. We have a thirst for movement, and we want our undertakings to involve resistance. The slouched man of the 1970s has been replaced by the man who stands up straight, who walks, projects himself, rides his bicycle. To be civilized today means recovering an energy that was lost through too much time spent in the seated position. Grandmothers dress up like long-distance runners, while granddads deck themselves out in hiking gear to go shopping or simply to cross the street. Tracksuits and trainers have become the new uniform for the white-haired tribe. They wear wings on their feet, but they have fragile legs supporting their shaky frames. Seniors take up their ski poles, anoraks, and sleeping bags, and set out on an endless race in the Olympic Games of time. They no longer resign themselves to their slippers and armchairs: the snobbery of being in good shape has reached every stage of life. People in their sixties today are pensioners who are high on vitamins, going through a feverish adolescence at an age when their ancestors were already senile or bedridden. Hiking trails are full of these snowy-maned adventurers, eager to bite off as much of existence as they can chew. I'm one of them, and I'm delighted by this reprieve that has been accorded to our kneecaps and lungs. The parts of the body no longer age at the same speed: age leaves its mark on our faces long before it affects anything else.

All the praise people heap on hiking today shouldn't fool us. The noble activity of hiking deteriorated during the pandemic into a sort of mania for oval tracks, for mechanical ambulation within a designated area. Millions of hamsters turned round and round in the courtyard of their prison. I love walking and I do it every day – I'm a compulsive pedestrian, regardless of the weather. But there exists a pathology of locomotion: vagrants and homeless people push their rags around in a shopping cart, condemned to perpetual wandering. For the American writer Henry David Thoreau, hero of modern ecology, this pathology even becomes an asceticism, the equivalent of a crusade. 'If you are ready to leave father and mother, and brother and sister, and wife and child and friends, and never see them again, – if you have paid your debts, and made your will, and settled all your affairs, and are a free man; then you are ready for a walk.'[2] This solitary man from Concord, Massachusetts, didn't follow his own precepts, because he never stopped taking refuge with his parents, and ended his bachelor's life alongside his sister. Nietzsche claimed to think with his feet. I see in this statement a slightly facile formulation that reminds me of François Mauriac's witticism about Michel Droit, the Gaullist member of the Académie française who shot himself in the foot during a safari: 'What will he write with now?' You never think during extreme physical effort – you just want to get to the top, with enough energy to go back down. Personally, I've never 'thought with my feet': I'm too busy wrapping them in bandages when a snug shoe or a bunched-up sock has wounded them, transforming them into conveyors of pain.[3] Allocating a brain to your feet is metaphorical acrobatics, nothing more. On a steep slope, I walk with my head down, not thinking about anything; to find a bit of relief, I count my steps to 500, then count them again. We attribute too many virtues to walking: going uphill is more sweating than meditating. And what about the cartilage pain it causes? Indeed, I might put it this way: walking is the curse of those who cannot die. The wandering Jew cannot lose his life because he has lost his death. The walking dead of the famous American series of that name are zombies who are condemned to turn in circles for the rest of time, in a constant state of hunger for human or animal flesh, until someone kills them a second time, this time for good. Not to mention those Alzheimer patients who flee their hospitals and wander about in a dazed and delirious state.

Toward the middle of the twentieth century a new generation of climbers appeared. Born of the counter-culture, at once relaxed and extremely bold, they were keen to break with the patriotic and puritanical morality of the mountain. James Salter's book *Solo Faces* deals beautifully with the mindset of this movement. Inspired by Gary Hemming (1934–69), that beatnik of the high peaks, the book tells the story of two friends from California, united by the same passion, who leave everything behind to go live in Chamonix and climb seemingly impossible rock faces before they eventually split up. They disobey rules, scoff at safety measures, and ask nothing of the authorities. For these quadrupeds of verticality, mountaineering is less a passion than an addiction, an uncontrollable gluttony of crests, walls, and ice. When the addiction dissipates, it leaves behind a taste of ashes. The main character, Rand, returns to an ordinary existence in California, with the terrible feeling that he is more alone than ever, still 'suspended in the void' between little and nothing. The mountain milieu, which has always been very masculine, has happily become more feminine. An ethics of competition has been replaced by an ethics of lightness.

Every walk and every climb begins in a store, and every sport has its uniform. We spend hours choosing the most comfortable shoes, the most practical pants or tights, the most up-to-date watch that shows you the altitude, your heart rate, and your lung capacity, the miniature backpack that contains everything essential in a small space, non-slip socks, and t-shirts that absorb sweat without retaining odours. Minor problems, at altitude, are the ultimate in major problems: a flask that hasn't been closed properly, a bag that's too heavy, or a shoe that's too small can destroy an expedition. There's a wide range of clothing choices, from the latest getup for hipsters who want to look like alpine hunters to outfits for reconstructed hippies whose only remaining trace of rebellion lies in their dreadlocks. Not to mention those high-altitude holiday destinations where chic and well-heeled style reigns: Austrian *lodens*, quilted jackets, sable coats, tapered ski pants, boots made of precious leather, mink hats. Even the huskies wrapped in Scottish plaids that you see on leashes in the streets of Megève, Gstaad, Davos, and Saint Moritz have changed their status: they've gone from being sled dogs to chubby lap dogs, trained for window shopping. The poor little darlings now have to watch their levels of fat and cholesterol.

What really stands out in this universe, especially in the summer, are the shorts people wear, especially the very tight and revealing shorts worn by women: it's the emancipation of the body in the interests of coquetry. There's an entire subtle hierarchy at play behind an apparent uniformity: a shirt left unbuttoned through a skilful negligence; an exposed bellybutton pierced by a gold ring; tattered Bermuda shorts with holes in all the right places; expensive brand-name shoes that denote membership in one tribe or another. The main thing you see when you climb are calves in every size and shape, clean-shaven or hairy, thick or slender, that invite you to follow them; I've surprised myself several times in my jealousy of the calves of my companions. Personally, my legs are as thin as matches. I've always envied the steady cadence of guides: they advance as though they were walking on an invisible staircase. Men also wear shorts: I once saw a womanizing grandpa with bird-like legs start chatting up a woman in her fifties who was lost on an immense firn near the Moëde-Anterne mountain hut and put her back on the right track – his own. After all, you have to respect the kindness of those hikers who help you and give you advice in a sort of instantaneous complicity. There's an English-speaking feminist who explains that women on mountain paths are constrained, and take on the appearance of nuns with big shoes, ugly hats, and tedious walking sticks.[4] I can attest that the opposite has been true for at least twenty years: I've never seen so many beautiful people in our mountains, wearing seductive outfits made of fine material that sometimes allows you to discern the outlines of the enigmatic tattoos beneath – they're as free in their appearance as they are in their minds, and what's more, they're gifted rock climbers. As for the grannies of my age, they're hotshot climbers who overtake stragglers with a laugh; anyone who sees them climb a wall like a spider can have no doubt that the world has changed. Dreaming about these women who climb gives you vital psychological fuel, even if today's decorum only allows you to say: I admire your ankles.

Part of the wonder of mountains is how they allow for a baroque juxtaposition of styles: from those nostalgic retired soldiers with their steady gait who pass you without even looking at you, to the unavoidable summer vacationers, wearing tank tops and flip flops at 2,500 metres, who inevitably take a wrong turn, get lost, and end up calling the rescue squad when they can't find their way. In 2016, on Mount Bégo (2,876 metres) in the Mercantour range, we picked up a family from Nice who had gotten lost in the fog and who, armed with an iPad that they brandished like the Eucharist, were looking for the parking lot where they'd left their car: the three children were wearing trainers, while the parents had on casual sneakers and polo shirts. All on his own, the oldest boy, barely twelve, who'd been sent out as a scout in advance of this party of the lost, repeated over and over with a rebellious weariness: my parents are idiots, my parents are idiots. Our guide, François Leray, forbade them from turning back on the pretext that they could topple into a ravine, and laboriously hauled them over the screes – by way of an exceptionally exposed final ridge – and up to the summit. The mother thanked him profusely as she condemned her 'fool of a husband' and squeezed him against her with an almost embarrassing ardour that would have led to something more had they been alone.

A question to no one in particular: why are female caretakers of mountain huts so sexy in the summer? I don't know whether it's an effect of the altitude or a mirage, but no sooner do our eyes light upon a feminine face than they draw comfort from it. Choosing young people to reinvigorate an exhausted pack of climbers is wise. The dirty and dishevelled hermits of yesteryear are no more. These diligent hostesses are muses for the visitors: they feed them and nourish their dreams; the climbers bring their face and their smile with them on the rock faces, like an encouragement that allows them to brave their fear. And if these caretakers also have the wisdom to play music of quality, they win the hearts of all. In another life, I'd love to be a warden for a season, from May to September, so as to welcome visitors, offering them shelves full of good books and beautiful music and playing films for them.

Mountain huts: whether they're ramshackle cabins or futuristic constructions perched at the foot of a moraine and jutting out over an ice tongue, they're the closest thing to a barn for humans, even if the newer establishments are more comfortable, sometimes providing single bedrooms. In the twentieth century, most of the tourists were kitted out like they'd just arrived from Club Med; today, many of them look like they've just escaped from a yoga class. You'd think you were in a Tibetan monastery: everyone meditates before setting out. Everyone's allowed a hot-water shower of four minutes, strictly timed. As soon as you enter the hut, you have to put on a pair of horrid rubber slippers. Meals are heavy and sometimes excellent, and their noisy conviviality makes you think of a boarding school. Most mountain huts are somewhere between a barracks and a second-class sleeping car; their character is at once rustic and temporary. You're not there to sleep but to await the next day, forced to lie down in a sort of litter in the middle of strangers who toss about, snore, point their headlamps toward you when they turn their heads, and start getting ready to leave at 2 a.m. The experience you have there is one of robust insomnia, reinforced by the fear of not being up to the next day's glaciers or walls. The most important thing is not to misplace any of your belongings, because it will be dark when you leave. If you have the misfortune of having to satisfy a need during the night, the walk to the lavatories is not unlike an expedition. And when the lavatories are outside – you can find them by their smell – you shiver with happiness in the lovely weather at 2,700 metres, seeing the spectral brilliance of the moon on the glaciers, or the dance of shadows on the rock faces of the mountains. They say that clumsy people, incapable of finding their way and deceived by the darkness, sometimes fall into the void. It's an end that's as horrific as it is ridiculous: dying is difficult enough without making everyone laugh when you do it.

The ordeal of the mountain hut distracts us from the fear of the next day like a diversion from difficulty. It's a nervous army that sets off early in the morning with tense faces, clearing out in a few minutes so they can get where they're going without having to wait behind other parties of mountaineers. When you return that afternoon, you have the feeling that it's all been worth it. Standing with your cheeks puffed out, you admire the paragliders you see out over the plain in the distance, as they rise and fall with the wind like notes in a musical score. The drone of a helicopter reassures you; you hear the whistle of a glider as it slips past overhead. You've forgotten your vertigo and all the hardships of the ascent: you've passed the test, and you're dazzled by the wonders you've glimpsed; even the terrible snorer of the night before, whose nasal tremors attacked your eardrums, has become a sort of accomplice – especially because you'll never see him again.

There's one essential character in these high-mountain ascents that I haven't dealt with yet: the guide, who can very quickly become a friend, a confidant as well as an instructor, especially if he's well-read and if conversation with him flows easily. Part shaman, part intercessor, he doesn't distinguish egotism from altruism, our security from his own. There's nothing better than climbing under the tutelage of an elder who protects us from ourselves, scolds us when we falter, encourages us when we do well. He meets our panic with a politics of calm, a pedagogical composure. A good guide is understated: he minimizes difficulties, and can even cause concern by trying to be too reassuring. But for a poltroon such as myself – I approach certain corridors like I've been sentenced to death – it's the only thing that works. When the weather gets bad or when difficulties pile up, the guide makes it clear that we're to obey his words to the letter. He goes from talkative to taciturn, sparing with his words; when the climb's over, we're never sure exactly what kind of danger we've escaped from.

Traditionally, mountaineering has been seen as a right-wing, aristocratic practice, while the left has championed hiking, which seems more closely linked with the people. The climber is a loner who only recognizes as equals the small number of 'happy few' who reach the heights like him. If he is the first in a rope team, he feels responsible for his companions. In this ultra-selective milieu that is based on the values of courage and abnegation, there is one category of climbers that sets itself apart: that of nonchalant prodigies, those masters of the cracks, men or women, who refuse to adulterate their path with anchors – nuts or cams, hexes or pegs – seeking instead to wed themselves to the rock like poets.[5] No more spiked shoes, steel-toed boots, or other climbing footwear; no more made-to-measure clothing in the latest style. Instead, it is an ethics of indifference that reigns, especially among the young. They dress up to look like hobos, clothed any old way – vagabonds straight out of Rimbaud. Light and slender as a cat, carrying a sachet instead of a backpack, they don't climb: they casually run through the air. It's amazing to see them setting out in the morning, ropes coiled around their shoulders as if they were going out to tame a stallion, the jingle of kitchenware and multi-coloured utensils hanging from snap hooks at their sides, with an obvious nonchalance that is the height of elegance. They're scruffy princes who make luxury of their pauperism. They practise an ostentatious frugality, refusing the heavy gear of their elders to climb in shorts and low-cut shoes. They finish in a few hours what would take you two whole days, and consider the most vertiginous climbs to be easy. They overtake you on walls with smiles on their faces, stepping across the steepest of inclines. They're marked by an asceticism of discretion, combining elegance with incredible power and imagining themselves to be bounding ibexes. Since they're young, in general good-looking, and astound you with their ease, you look at them with envy – especially if you yourself have been exiled from the land of youth.

Two desires of equal strength combat one another in these people: that of allegiance and that of dissidence. In their age, their clothing, and their physical fitness, they belong to a specific generation – from which they nonetheless seek to distinguish themselves. You leave a certain fellowship around the age of thirty, when life pulls immortality out from under your feet, and pushes you toward the creation of a family and the entrance into adulthood. What reigns in all these groups is the frantic quest for that little something that will distinguish you from those around you. With this ironic consequence: the heresy of the innovators always becomes the orthodoxy of those who succeed them. Indifferent to today's fashions, they create those of tomorrow. These young people are at once aristocrats in their bearing and romantics in their desire for originality. Departing from well-trodden paths, the alternatives they create will nonetheless be added to – and thereby enrich – the catalogue of routes that are possible. Every scout is a prospector.

CHAPTER 8

# The Two Faces of the Abyss

That fizzing, nauseous, faintly erotic feeling of real terror.

ROBERT MACFARLANE[1]

The mountain remains a hostile place. Whether we like it or not, we walk in the footsteps of possible death when we walk upon it. She crouches in ambush behind every ascent. A single slip, a false step, a little pebble in the wrong place, and a fall – with drastic consequences – is inevitable. I remember an old philosopher, lover of the open air, who told us how, during an easy descent in the Savoie, his legs suddenly failed him and cast him into a trench where he broke several bones. In one way or another, every tricky ascent brings you face to face with the abyss: you inhale it, you repel it. There are two forms of vertigo: the uncontrollable whirling of those who are affected by the void, even when they're sitting on a stool; and a more metaphysical vertigo – the idea that a single forward step might cast us into the abyss. This is the vertigo of an infinite freedom that can choose to die right then and there. I own my death – it depends on me alone – and I can either bring it about or push it away. This temptation of falling is above all a nightmare: you imagine your body dropping into a precipice and bouncing off the rocks; it takes a moment and a few shivers before you get a grip on yourself. Falling is fatal, so you have to make it impossible. Every metre won is a foiled catastrophe, but every difficulty you overcome causes you to lose a bit of vigilance, making an eventual accident possible. Bachelard speaks somewhere about Thomas de Quincey and the illness of the abyss, that dread of endlessly falling, thereby creating the very chasms we fear. You never return from that fall that comes back to you in dreams.

*Great Fear on the Mountain*: this is the title of a very beautiful novel by Charles Ramuz in which the characters are proper names without any real personalities, because the mountain is the sole subject of the narration. She is the one who sees and decides everything, who lays down the law; men are nothing more than impotent witnesses to her will. She is at once magnificent and maleficent. In certain high valleys, the sun disappears from October to April, making the scenery lugubrious. People therefore worry that the light won't return, and that snow will block all the roads, cutting the inhabitants off from the world outside. Conversely, I sometimes imagine, when I go to bed at night, that the mountain ranges will vanish as a result of the darkness. What would people say if, in the morning, the most important summits had been cleared from the ground the same way you clear the table? The mountain is treacherous even when she seems to smile upon us, and she is never as deceitful as when the sun is shining. She welcomes us without tolerating us. Her risks cannot be avoided; indeed, we invite these risks just as we fear them. This is the psychological baggage of the hiker. As we've always known, courage does not mean being unaware of danger, but overcoming fear – this is the only thing that matters. You have to be able to suppress your adrenaline and the uncontrollable trembling to which it leads, especially during tricky passages.

Climbing enlists several contradictory resources: precaution and boldness; the art of advancing on uncertain terrain combined with the will to overcome obstacles. You need that virtue that the English call 'grit':[2] the ability to brave adversity without complaining. On the mountain, you're always exchanging one worry for another: a considered will to advance versus an irrational reflex to panic. The first is a cold calculation of the perils, the second is terror in the face of the slope. Foresight must work hand in hand with confidence, for all it takes is a falling rock, a poorly tied knot, or a poorly buckled harness for everything to fall apart. At which point arises the pure panic that is born of an undesired possibility: it depends on me to ensure that everything depends on me, that I'm not thrown to my death. I hold my life in my hands: if I teeter, I kill myself. This delicate position of being right on the edge of the void generally produces the effect of a jolt, giving the arms and legs the impetus required to keep climbing. In a like manner, every slip and every loose rock leads us to imagine their possible consequences and hence to tremble. I've missed falling onto the rocks below by a hair, and in my imagination I see myself lying down there twitching, my bones broken in a thousand places. What would happen if I were skiing and the earth vanished beneath my feet; what would happen if a patch of unstable snow carried me away? If the guide of our rope team keeled over and fell into a crevasse, leaving the rest of us stranded? He can very well explain to us how the radio works, but we still have the confused feeling that without him we'd be incapable of calling for help.

We all know about 'tornado hunters', those kamikazes who enjoy putting themselves – often by piloting small aeroplanes – right in the eye of the storm, in that place where everything is calm even though the storm rages all around. Any rock climber is familiar with the way fear increases the emotional charge of an ascent. To confront a steep incline, a treacherous ridge, or a baritone-voiced wind that knocks you down like a bowling pin is to overcome what threatens to slay you. Every minute is a door at which death can knock; every false step is a potential collapse. But without the fear of plummeting, nothing's at stake. As Robert Macfarlane says, 'we never feel so alive as when we have nearly died'.[3] To speak of an accident from which you escaped is to speak of a miracle, that of survival. Through words, you exorcise the peril you've overcome. Instinctively, we find great heights intimidating. But we humanize even the most forbidding rock faces when we approach them and embark upon their ascension. The rock is that adversary that I must turn into a friend; it is a palimpsest that I must decipher like a page of braille, one that demands to be read by my fingertips as much as my eyes. The novice who zips up every overhang, who hugs those places on the rock wall that good climbers avoid, has forgotten the most important principle: that of finding a balance point between two grips, of calmly seeking out a step or a projection that will help him to progress. What does it mean to be a beginner at the age of seventy? Does it make you desperate, sad? Or, on the contrary, does it make you an eternal neophyte who tries new things and continues to progress at an age when others sit in their wheelchairs?

Fear can immobilize a climber who has lost the physical resources he needs to keep going: this is the stunned horror of the amateur who is blocked on a path, incapable of going up or down – stuck to the rock. His friends or his guide can try all they want to persuade him, to encourage him to get out of his predicament. His fear of death increases with each passing moment. You have to plan for the worst to be able to avoid it. We can hear in these words an echo of the Stoic practice of *praemeditatio*, whereby one anticipates potential bad occurrences so as to thwart them. For Seneca, depriving yourself of food and drink and wilfully exposing yourself to afflictions means mitigating the shock of these ordeals when they end up happening. It gives us the experience of misfortune in homeopathic doses. A mountaineer must be able to react to the unexpected – storms that come out of nowhere, with their pale light that carves into rocks, giving them a yellowish tint; ice axes that sizzle along the surface instead of stopping your slide. During a *tour de France des frontières* (in which one completes an entire turn around France by following its borders), as he traversed the crests of the Rois Mages between France and Italy, Lionel Daudet was electrocuted, after hearing the sound of the drone of bees that is a tell-tale sign of impending lightning. The bolt pierced him from the bottom of his back to the ends of his toes. 'I had the feeling I was paralyzed, that I was a glass statue that had broken into pieces.'[4] He survived, but the bolt left a round scar at the base of his vertebral column the size of a two-euro coin. He thinks his life was saved by the ice axe that was hanging from his bag, without which the electrical arc would have entered by way of his head, thereby killing him. An immense flash of lightning is a bomb exploding above you. There's another beautiful story of a man struck by lightning, recounted by Oliver Sacks in his book *Musicophilia*. In 1994, a certain Tony Cicoria, a forty-two-year-old orthopaedic surgeon, is inside a phone booth in Albany in the middle of a storm when a bolt strikes him. He survives, despite a heart attack, but a short time afterwards finds that he is possessed of a violent desire to play the piano and buy sheets on which to write music. Hearing notes in his head, he sets down to compose them, and becomes an excellent musician. He was struck by a love of music as if by lightning; I almost envy him this fertile accident, one that led to so much creation. The sky's artillery transformed him – not into a genius, perhaps, but at least into an artist. In a short story called 'Le Poids du papillon', Erri De Luca, that Franciscan of the peaks, speaks of a chamois who, plagued by stings and bites as a storm approaches, suddenly feels its fur standing on end, and fleas being splattered at great speed. A magnificent metaphor: electrostatic tension swept away his parasites.

You can think about fear, but fear isn't something that is thought. It joins the subject to the object of his terror. It numbs the body and the mind, thus giving rise to the very mishaps from which it was supposed to protect us. Good fear, on the contrary, makes us more alert, allows us to avoid fatal mistakes, and stimulates our psychological abilities. In extreme circumstances, it drives us to build improvised bivouacs in the middle of a storm, to make emergency descents when the racket of unleashed elements goes off. Healthy fear energizes; harmful fear paralyses.

Mountains are beautiful because they resist us. Where are my limits? asks the climber, who takes pleasure in verifying these limits or even pushing them back. This is how we should understand those people in their fifties, sixties, and beyond who run, hike, climb. They're driven by the desire to not give up the ghost; they annoy those who are younger than them, for they're in the state known as *the pathos of obstinacy*.[5] As they climb, their old resentments dissipate; they reconcile themselves with nature and men, and rediscover an innocence they thought they'd lost. While many associate age with decline – especially as concerns those over fifty – I see it as a last chance, a crowning moment of possibility. 'Having your entire life behind you – that's when you're truly free', said a young J. M. G. Le Clézio in 1963. My wager is the opposite, that of having a life before me to the very end, of enjoying a freedom that, far from being austere, seeks to take on new challenges and to take joy in facing the world. The desire to broaden your existence grows as the existence in question fades away. There are two kinds of beings: those who are exhausted by the act of living, and those who are astounded by an overabundance of energy, even if they only have an hour left to live. Those who coop themselves up and those who expose themselves. And also two models of old age, one that is dynamic, the other that is entropic. The first offers itself up to the future, while the other turns toward the past and its nostalgia. The first undertakes projects, the other consumes itself in regrets.

The constraints we love most are the ones we impose upon ourselves with a view to attaining a higher objective. For the latter, we're willing to brave the worst dangers, to tolerate inhuman ordeals. Each person establishes his own personal scale of suffering, which he's willing to bear right up to the point of frostbite or, in the worst cases, amputation. In the words of Lionel Terray: 'With a few rare exceptions the climber has no renown to hope for, and no audience to encourage him apart from his companion on the rope. Alone among the silence and solitude of the mountains he fights for the joy of overcoming his chosen obstacle by his own unaided powers.'[6] The best test is the one you can convert into a power over yourself, into a personal account, into a challenge to your own finitude. This is the strange wager of the contemporary citizen: he seeks to wed heroism and will, and impose upon himself a surfeit of intentional peril. He opposes desirable sufferings to those that are inevitable, such as illness, mourning, and disappointment. Sometimes, when you dig deep within yourself, you find the strength of a stubborn mule who refuses to stop. The body is always too heavy, even when you're slender: its cumbersome weight is too much even when you imagine you're a bird. It discourages you and makes you stop. And then you keep going. Giving up would be degrading. Not everyone is a 'dancer playing with gravity',[7] as Lionel Terray said of Lachenal. Each climb is both spiritual and material: modest as the ascension may be, you feel transported for having done it, as though you'd touched something essential.

After a certain age, the mountain allows us to do only one thing: persevere. It's quite a risk to play the clown on a slab or do acrobatics on steep slopes. Our time bears witness to a strange division of labour: on the one hand, demands of victimhood are spreading like wildfire in our overprotected societies – there's a competition to see who can whine loudest; on the other hand, a growing number of men and women wear themselves out reaching the poles on sleds, crossing the ocean on boats little bigger than nutshells, swinging through the air on ropes. Agony may be our lot in life, but many people today turn this into a choice and even an object of faith, as though they were mocking our natural misery: up here, on mountain paths and crests, we're free to loosen the bonds that strangle us, and to choose which dangers we want to confront. Hikers and mountaineers who have kept company with a mountain for a long time are in fact engaged in a complex dialogue with it, for at some point it begins to return the love and the trust they place in it. It's as though the mountain had initiated them.

Mountain ranges and summits belong to those sacred spaces that impart a new art of living. It's enough to give us shivers. Like the sea, they offer to those who cherish them a daily transfiguration. Great rock faces bring those who desire them toward salvation. They are my road to redemption.

CHAPTER 9

# Reynard and Isengrim

Even a tame wolf never stops dreaming of the forest.

RUSSIAN PROVERB

What is savagery? It's the invention of a culture that seeks to rediscover, at its end point, that which it opposed at its origins. The bucolic, for instance, is the reconstruction of an idealized rural world. We lament the disappearance of this universe and its seasonal rhythms. Our very urban passion for local farm products should be seen from the standpoint of nostalgia; for nature, of its very essence, is that which has always been lost. Wooded groves and the simple life whose praises we sing were themselves fashioned from the hand of man. We project onto past times a purity that doesn't exist: there was never any dawn of the world; artifice began in the Neanderthal age, when the first farmers or breeders had to systematically exploit the land where they lived in order to survive. The reintroduction of the wolf and the lynx in the southeast, and bears and birds of prey in the Pyrenees, means our countryside is once more inhabited by dangerous powers. In the name of a new relationship with the living world, we restore the violence that our ancestors sought to eradicate, at the cost of an insurmountable dilemma. For about thirty years now, the civilized world, bored of comfort and safety, has promoted a Europe in which people are surrounded by wild animals. This mindset allows the authorities to reintroduce on the sly dangerous species; even worse, it demands their reintroduction, claiming that man is the only dangerous predator, the only barbarian who must be kept at bay. We invent concepts that would have caused an uproar among our ancestors: the friendly wolf, the nice bear. It's ethology according to Walt Disney. The historian Michel Pastoureau gently mocks those zoologists and defenders of wolves who maintain their harmlessness, trying to exonerate them of all the crimes of which they're accused.[1] This is dishonesty lined with ignorance, because records show that wolves attack humans and eat the corpses of soldiers on battlefields. They have entered Paris several times, in 1421 (a particularly terrifying year), 1423, and 1438; they again surrounded the capital in 1685 and 1710 during horrifically harsh winters.[2]

The truth is that wolves make people crazy – above all those who adore them – thus becoming objects of an almost fanatical indoctrination. This sentimental lupomania in fact arises from an unsuspecting anthropomorphism: people humanize animals to as to better animalize humans. In a similar vein, a petition to save rats made the rounds two years ago in Paris, arguing that we should consider them not as pests but as friends. In Strasbourg in February 2021, an environmentalist elected official suggested that we should see bedbugs and mice not as enemies but as mutually beneficial cohabitants to which we should adapt! Not only should we let wolves repopulate our countryside, we should also become wild animals, monkeys or great predators ourselves – in short, awaken the beast that sleeps within us. We owe this mythology of re-wilding to Jack London and his great novels, such as *The Call of the Wild* (1903) and *White Fang* (1906). In the former, Buck, a sled dog who is haunted by his origins, decivilizes himself, returns to his ancestors, and finds himself transformed into a demon made flesh. The wolf inside him is a deposed king who reclaims his title; his throat vibrates with the song of the pack; he rids himself of his domesticity; he remembers 'in vague ways ... the youth of his breed, ... the time the wild dogs ranged in packs through the primeval forest and killed their meat as they ran it down ... And when, on the still cold nights, he pointed his nose at a star and howled long and wolf-like, it was his ancestors, dead and dust, pointing nose at star and howling down through the centuries and through him.'[3] He has all the physical power of a king, 'mastered by the sheer surging of life, the tidal wave of being, the perfect joy of each separate muscle'.[4] As for White Fang, given over to 'a wistfulness bred of hunger',[5] he mercilessly hunts down his victim. At least Jack London harbours no illusions about this carnivore: it is brute force, controlled violence, that he celebrates by way of him. What he denounces, like many others of his time, is the anaesthesia of life brought about by a modern civilization founded on the crushing of instincts and the regimentation of freedom. This *Bildungsroman* calls for an unlearning, a life-saving regression.

In the nineteenth century, chamois, mountain sheep, and ibexes had virtually disappeared from France; in the twentieth century, they were found only in Switzerland, Austria, Bavaria, and the Dolomites. It's great to know that they're there once more, and in large numbers, in our mountain ranges. As a city dweller, I'm in favour of the return of wolves (and of bears in the Pyrenees) because it doesn't harm me, and I hunt out even the slightest trace of them on the trails. For the time being, you almost never see these stealthy animals, but you do come across the dismembered bodies they leave behind. The first one I saw was twenty years ago in Dormillouse, in the Hautes-Alpes, where reformists once sought refuge from Catholic persecution. It was the carcass of a sheep that had been torn open; its entrails were being devoured by flies. A pack had killed it without eating it, just to leave behind a trace of its feats. I've only come across a few wolves in my life: a pack of a dozen grey-furred individuals in Yellowstone Park in Wyoming, circling around a wounded bison they intended to kill; a very aggressive pair in Romania, in a semi-reserve near the city of Cristian in Transylvania. One January evening around 11, on a road in the Aravis Range, when we noticed three long silhouettes tirelessly climbing with beautiful strides; I remember the feeling of admiration that seized us at that moment.

The return of the wolf, which returned to the French Alps from Abruzzo in the 1990s, is the return of a medieval tremor to the twenty-first century, a pile-up of time periods, a mingling with carnivorous predators in a setting of winter sports. The fact that these animals were observed by telescope on the ski runs of the Courchevel in March 2020, and on Mont Joux above Megève in December of the same year, is evidence of a muted encirclement. Behind the familiar landscape of black or red ski runs and the basket chairlifts that swing in the wind, the marauder prowls, discreet yet present, like a shadow behind a screen that might emerge onto the stage at any moment. He amazes and terrifies wherever he goes; the power of his jaws is astounding; he can cover 100 kilometres a day; his intelligence throws hunters off course; shepherds dread him, and dream of being able to slaughter him when he attacks their herds. Dark emissary of the chthonic world of the Middle Ages, he's now the embodiment of a biodiversity in need of repair. Men reintroduce ibexes, mountain sheep, eagles, vultures, bearded vultures, bears, and lynx, seeking to recreate, by their will power alone, a cohabitation that will hopefully be peaceful, an earthly paradise from after the Fall. This all assumes a sudden wisdom on the part of nature, which would contain within itself an innate sense of balance. There's something to the argument: the reintroduction of the fox, for example, leads to the elimination of voles, which devour crops. But a great many other species are already proliferating – roe deer, white-tailed deer, and above all boar – without being regulated, other than by hunters and hunting organizations. In other words, our legitimate concern for living beings resembles a pile of contradictory interests and desires: we reintroduce the wolf in complete disregard for farmers and shepherds, whom we sacrifice to the latest pro-animal fad.

What is the wolf today? A battle of ideas between the partisans and adversaries of the canine. With every massacre of sheep, lambs, or goats, the fight starts up again, and farmers threaten to take up arms if the state doesn't do what's necessary. In 1995, for example, after numerous attacks on herds followed by a demonstration by farmers and exasperated elected officials, a bridge was blown up along the Vésubie in the Alpes-Maritimes department. Responsibility for the attack was claimed by the 'Brothers of the Wolves', who excoriated what they called the 'shitty hunters'.[6] The carcass of a wolf riddled with buckshot was found in the Mercantour National Park, and the Minister of the Environment at the time, Corinne Lepage, condemned what she called a 'homicidal act'. We can add to this imbroglio the fierce hostility of the Greens toward hunters, whom they want to ban from the public sphere, and whom they consider veritable terrorists. (Recall that on 21 January 2021, environmentalist elected officials brought flowers to pay their respects to a young stag who was tracked by hunters right to the Chantilly train station. People were outraged by their homage, a parody of ceremonies held for victims of terrorism.) Everywhere in France over the last thirty years, ovines, and at times young bulls and heifers, have been decimated by wolves, aggravating tensions even though the government allows officials from hunting clubs to kill a certain number of them each year. Like every city dweller, I have a romantic fascination with wolves. While dogs bark stupidly, the wolf vocalizes and howls, its noise pointed toward the sky so that it can be heard for miles around. According to the musicologist André Manoukian, wolves even invented choral singing. And we're right to be fascinated by their fiery v-notched eyes, and their nocturnal vision (they can supposedly see in the dark), which speak of instinct – the instinct to kill. It's a cold beauty that, rather than watching you, watches itself contemplate the world.

Speaking to shepherds who summer in the Mercantour changes your perspective: they understand the skill of these killers, and many demand the right to slaughter them if they roam too close to their enclosures, just as other shepherds in Aubrac seek to frighten away scavengers. No fewer than 1,200 sheep were killed by wolves in 2020 in the Hautes-Alpes alone! They worry that these predators might one day carry off a child. The generous subsidies given by the state and the European Union in no way mollify the legitimate anger of shepherds and goatherds, who experience each attack as a personal wound. The pastoral economy is not very compatible with the presence of wolves in the Alps and bears in the Pyrenees, which sometimes causes dozens of panicked ovines to leap into chasms. Let's be honest: a hiker has more chance of being bitten by a sheepdog – a Great Pyrenees, a Beauceron, a Malinois – than by a wolf. But we're often closer than we think to a fatal accident, and the first time a child or an adult is wounded by a wolf, ancestral fear will rear its head once more (in December 2020 in the Isère, a pack was able to cut a young bull weighing 250 kilos to pieces). Our policy concerning the reintroduction of wild species is an incoherent mishmash whereby the state tries to mediate between two hostile parties, at the risk of being beaten on all sides.

The bleating flocks of animals in their thousands that move toward alpine pastures every spring resembles a river that turns back to its source. Sheep, goats, ewes advance in unruly hordes, driven forth by hyperactive dogs who bite those who stray. In comparison with this vagrant herd, slowed by its sheer number, wolves seem like guerrillas organized into mobile and perfectly disciplined commando units. The caprine army is unified by nothing more than fear and mimicry. When a carnivore appears, or merely howls, panic reigns among the future prey. They turn in circles, or sometimes dash in a single movement toward the enemy, perfectly illustrating Kant's dictum: 'Fear is absurd because it brings about the very thing it wants to avoid.' People in the Hautes-Alpes tell the story of an extraordinary event that happened some time ago. A flock of sheep and goats had been placed in a wire-mesh enclosure to ensure their safety. In the middle of the night, the wolves arrive. They howl and wake the flock. Terrified, the sheep and goats begin to move in circles, and then, realizing they are confined, start to plough into the fence with their heads. The wolves get even louder, causing the terrified ovines to focus their efforts on a specific part of the enclosure. Due to their great numbers, they finally succeed in breaking down the fence that's protecting them, and leave their pen en masse. All that's left is for the wolves to help themselves – the sheep have collaborated in their own elimination. It's total carnage: there are only a few animals who are not slaughtered, or who do not throw themselves from a cliff with a frightening swiftness. The predators have other ruses as well: sometimes one or two of them (often she-wolves in heat) will get the attention of the sheepdogs, making them run for several kilometres while their peers decimate the plump beasts and relish the feast.

There are two sides to the wolf, one real, the other imaginary; it's this latter side that is defended by its partisans, who rarely have to deal with its bad manners. While they cherish the wolf like a chimera, shepherds and watchmen are subjected to its reality. A 'wolf certification label' has even been created in a theme park dedicated to wolves in Saint-Martin-Vésubie; in an ironic twist, breeders have adapted it as a seal of quality to sell their lamb – as though it were endorsed by the killers.[7] This fragile framework is held in place at the expense of the locals. At the heart of a certain mythology, the wolf figures as an enchanting emblem, while the bear, though it is just as dangerous, remains locked within a childish imagery (a masterly exception to this rule is the work of the anthropologist Nastassja Martin, whose jaw was torn off by a bear in Siberia, and who considered herself to be inhabited by the spirit of her attacker, as if she were a half-woman, half-bear hybrid[8]). The teddy bear has killed the grizzly, and so it is the canine, Jack London's magnificent brute, that adventurers treasure. For them, we're all domesticated wolves – we should break our chains and howl with rage at the stars. (The wolfdog, for its part, has all the ferocity of the wolf but none of its nobility; it is the lost offshoot of a poorly domesticated breed.) In the wild, it's kill or be killed; either you eat or you're eaten, for as London wrote, 'the aim of life was meat'.[9] The activists tell us that we should all reconnect with our wild nature – our 'wilderness', as they say in English, which is 'a place of healing for our sick psyches and bodies'.[10] What are we to understand by this? Reconnecting with natural rhythms and living in the countryside, or revitalizing violence, the transgression of laws, the refusal to obey rules? By reintroducing wild animals alongside classic human activities, we create a synthetic mountain, just as agribusiness multinationals produce synthetic meat under the pretext of fighting the slaughter of animals. It's not the mountain of yesteryear – it's an entirely new mountain. As such, we find Mongolian yurts and llamas when we climb in the Alps, just as we find palm trees in Brittany, and parakeets from the Indies in Parisian parks, chasing away the sparrows and chickadees. In Megève they've even transplanted bison – at 2,000 metres. In July 2019, nineteen of these creatures who had escaped their pen (they're raised for their meat) on Mont Joux were killed in the interests of safety on the orders of the prefecture, in a gesture at once absurd and cruel. The transplantation of untamed species is not always a good thing. Even donkeys and mules, once referred to as 'ministers of seasonal migration' for traders and smugglers, today carry suitcases, bags, or children for visiting travellers. The army of equids goes hand in hand with that of tourists.

There are many interactions between humans and wild animals, and they're often surprising: ibexes and marmots sometimes become less timid and approach people who walk by. I recall a bold marmot in the Vanoise National Park who set himself down right beside the path, licking the arms, hands, and feet of the volunteers to reap the salt of their sweat. I qualified for his rough solicitude on my calves, knees, and one of my palms. He carried out this task with diligence, making the children burst out laughing. (Learning later on that this burrowing mammal digests his food twice by ingesting a portion of his faeces cooled my enthusiasm.) The return to nature also entails the possible perversion of wild animals, who are tempted to look for food near humans. Don't people talk about 'spaghetti wolves' in the Abruzzo, who search out restaurant 'leftovers', just as there are 'pizza bears' in the Rockies, who conscientiously empty out the trash cans? I remember a cabin I rented in Yosemite Park in the 1980s, while I was teaching in San Diego: I forgot to lock the door, and we were awakened at night by a tremendous racket – the kitchen was occupied by a good-sized brown bear who was trying to open the fridge. Our screams chased him off, and I immediately felt bad for not having left him a honey pot as a consolation. The best place to find bears in Colorado or New Mexico is the local dump. In Alaska, Siberia, and all over the Arctic, polar bears, suffering from a reduction in their hunting territory and their own overpopulation, are increasingly coming closer to human settlements. At the same time, in France, we see a proliferation of pillaging deer and boar. Wandering cows spread panic in Corsica. In a seaside resort there, young boars have been found living in hairdryers in a beauty salon and running along the beach in the midst of holidaymakers. In Italy, they invade cities in the hundreds of thousands.

This is the ambiguity of our reparations: history never goes backwards. The nature to which we want to give back its rights is never anything more than a reconstruction of culture, even if, in Abruzzo or Spain, cohabitation between domestic and wild species seems to have been managed better than in France. The symbolism of the wolf won't disappear anytime soon, for it touches upon an obvious form of human mimicry, as seen in the example of those North American survivalists who, afraid of being emasculated by an overly feminine culture, hide in forests, disguising themselves as trappers or Indians by covering themselves in animal hides so as to awaken the beast within. In an excellent graphic novel by Jean-Marc

Rochette, an exhausted hunter is saved by a wolf he wanted to kill, who shares the carcass of a chamois with him.[11] Is this an example of 're-wilding'? The return to raw meat as a key to reconciliation? Are we going to celebrate the way a peaceful walker begins to transform himself into a wolf by liberating his instincts (including the most violent ones), eating raw meat, and walking on all fours? Or the way forest lovers seek to become deer, in a new-age version of Bambi?[12] Who are these superior beings who present themselves as ambassadors of wild fauna and seek to cut humans down to size?[13] Who use the grizzly, the wolf, and the lynx to beat up the human race? (Modern mountain men are wilfully sententious.) This neo-savagism still belongs to the dreams of civilized people who idealize nature and trees so as to pamphleteer against the modern world. They want to return to the origins of humanity, refusing to acknowledge that history has happened in the meantime. Post-civilization savagery is in no way foreign to civilization. And we mustn't forget those proselytizing vegans who would like to re-educate carnivorous species, forcing wolves, dogs, coyotes, and lynx to eat fruit and vegetables: the animalism of these people reaches the very heights of human imperialism. When we see wolves wandering on highways or approaching villages, we should no longer speak of the infusion of nature, but of confusion. In an interesting reversal, we speak of a return to natural life when in fact we should speak of a domestication of alterity: mountains and the fauna that lives there are indifferent to our principles. We still seek in them the negation of our own values, a rectification of that which is harmful in our societies. We think we're making changes to ourselves, but we're just projecting; we believe we're loosening our grip on something we're in fact colonizing. I take great pleasure from Samivel, who, borrowing from medieval fabliaus, reverses their clichés in his illustrated works about Reynard and Isengrim: the fox becomes a trickster and a smooth-talker, while the wolf is awkward and foolish. Famished, he loses his teeth, and has to play the minstrel so someone will give him a bowl of soup.

A beautiful example of sensitivity: disoriented on a difficult ascent in the Mont Blanc massif, at an altitude of 3,000 metres, Walter Bonatti notices a dying butterfly on the snow; the warmth of the day had carried it to these heights in a sort of ecstasy of ascension. He takes it in his hand, shields it from the elements, and brings it down to the Charpoua mountain hut (2,841 metres), at the foot of the Drus.[14]

# CHAPTER 10

# Loving What Terrifies Us

*That is sublime in comparison with which everything else is small.*

IMMANUEL KANT[1]

When I was a child, whenever we drove toward Les Houches, the Bossons Glacier had the courtesy to stop barely a kilometre from the road, its lower lip planed so as to let the traffic pass. At least that's how I like to remember it. It was a waterfall of cotton that descended and turned into logs, stones, dust. Its dirty muzzle, composed of pine trees, crushed rocks, and ground up snow terrified me. It became diluted a little further down, turning into muddy streams and flooding the road on the hottest days. Its nasty face seemed to say: next time, I'm going to submerge you. But in fact it's the opposite that happened: we're the ones who chase after glaciers to save them. In Switzerland, they're wrapped in coverings to protect them from the sun's radiation: it's no longer a fast-flowing river begot by the mountains to cover the valleys, but a thwarted foetus returning to its birthplace. (The Bossons Glacier retreated in the 1940s, and then recovered its losses between 1955 and 1990, crushing the trees and bushes that had colonized the walls at its sides. It has been shrinking again since that time.) All that's left today are a few kilometres of moraine. For a long time I found glaciers terrifying, but now I've begun to worry for them. These immense machines that flatten mountains are slow-motion torrents, giant sanders that have done their work over the course of centuries, indeed millennia. There's something digestive about this phenomenon, which is like the entrails of a huge intestine that spews its waste across valleys, here and there leaving erratic blocks, those rocks sheathed in yellow like the remains of buttered bread. In winter, the glacier, covered in snow, looks like a pastry with multiple cones and an anarchic dentition. It's like a vanilla coulis that's been poured onto a cake: it almost looks varnished. In the summer, it's more like a big dirty lizard covered in wrinkles and folds, a procession of dust and broken wood. Starting from the end of June, this sea of ice even takes on the appearance of a very old crocodile that has emerged from the mud and is still covered in earth. The glacier that had previously eroded stone is now eroded by it, and looks monstrously destitute. The stone eats it, almost grazing on it as it climbs back up toward its source. I can still see the last glacier of Mercantour, the Clapier, from up above in the summer: it looks like the remains of a prehistoric animal, grey and crumpled.

There's another fabulous aspect of this congealed river: its power of conservation. Like the unconscious, it seems unaware of time, but possesses a staggering memory: it forgets nothing, restoring the slightest thing that it entrusted to it, even thirty or fifty years later. It's a veritable family novel of nature. This labyrinth of frozen passageways, dungeons, and secret chambers is always ready to swallow what falls into it. It's a stomach that, rather than digesting, safeguards everything it swallows. The blue walls of its icy intestines conserve everything at low speeds. If you throw precious jewels or an attractive watch into a crevasse today, they'll still be intact for your great-grandchildren. They'll be caught in a subtle vice, not one of death but of life in slow motion, an organic process that stretches out across decades. We know the story of the *Malabar Princess*, the plane belonging to an Indian airline that flew between Bombay and London via Geneva, and crashed into the Bossons Glacier on 3 November 1950 at 4,677 metres, on the rocky point known as the Tournette. There were no survivors. In a horrific coincidence, or perhaps a curse, another Air India plane, the *Kangchenjunga*, crashed at practically the same site in 1966, causing the death of 117 passengers, one of whom was a famous Indian physicist. In the time since, the glacier has ceaselessly rendered hands, feet, jewels, dried bones, precious stones, and fragments of the aeroplane, some of which it transformed into metal sculptures. There was even a diplomatic suitcase full of documents and newspapers. Nothing ages in the cold except skin, which cracks. (The sonority of the name 'Malabar Princess' is troubling. It makes us think of a young royal with an athletic physique, or a teenager blowing bubbles with her chewing gum.) In 1833, Charles Darwin, driving a team of mules across the Portillo snowfields (in the Andes, at 2,870 metres), discovered that 'on one of these columns of ice a frozen horse was exposed, sticking as on a pedestal, but with its hind legs straight up in the air'.[2] The glacier had swallowed it and embalmed it. (The theme of the horse, or of mummified remains in seracs, has become a topos of the modern detective novel, in the work, for example, of Bernard Minier and Jean-Christophe Grangé.) Like those mountaineers found embedded in a translucent block of ice, or standing stiffly in a carapace on a ledge with their ice axe. We might think of the Grevin Museum – a wax museum in Paris – as dedicated to glaciers.

The vaults that glaciers comprise attract grave robbers. They return corpses with the precision of a notary: a guide from Chamonix discovered the body of his grandfather fifty years after his death; in 2017, the bodies of a couple who had departed from Chandolin (in the canton of Valais) in 1942 to feed their cattle were discovered in the Diablerets, along with sleeping bags, a bottle, a book, and a watch. In 2016, the remains of a mercenary who had died around 1600, along with his sword, pistol, and some coins, emerged on the Theodul Pass in Switzerland. A year later, beneath the Dômes de Miage in the Mont Blanc massif, three German mountaineers who vanished in the 1990s reappeared. In 2014, a father was informed that the body of his son, an aspiring guide who had set out thirty-two years earlier to climb the Aiguille Verte, had been discovered; the father had been dreading this discovery, and it deeply saddened him: he would have preferred for his son to remain up above, 'in his kingdom'. The cold had grasped them all in a horrifying embrace. The rise in temperatures has accelerated the discovery of the missing; from now to the end of the century, we should expect hundreds of corpses to be exhumed.

Long forsaken, glaciers are now fawned upon, tended to like porcelain. Nothing combines beauty and difficulty like walking on their surface – it's like tickling the back of a dragon who will snatch you in its jaws at the slightest hint of carelessness. In such moments, the glacier vacuums you up through a process of suction; the earth vanishes, and woe to the one who is not roped to others. You need only glance at the marvellous horror of the glacier's chasm to imagine it tearing you to shreds. You have to avoid putting too much weight on the arcs formed by the snow during the warmest hours of the day. This is not even to mention the seracs suspended overhead, each of which is the equivalent of a five- or six-ton truck with its wheels hanging over the edge of a cliff, threatening to tip over at any moment. Seen from afar, a glacier looks like a staircase of white marble; its slopes are majestic, especially after a snowfall – it is as though a queen had come down from the heavens, announcing her presence with an extravagant procession. Seen from up close, it's a warped ship, a chaotic mass of cubes, shards, and spears several metres in length – a deceptively calm petrified swell emitting worrying gurgles and, at times, the crash of a falling block of ice. In the strong heat of the summer, glaciers undergo a significant ablation at their surface: they display their raw gums like sneering skeletons exhumed from a grave. A glacier is anything but silent: it cracks and moans everywhere as if it were a complex horological mechanism. In good weather you can hear it singing, especially if you're near its randklufts: waters that had been held captive awaken and begin to prattle and gab all along the slope. Springs, henceforth separated, now converge. Crevasses look like purplish-blue mouths revealing gigantic cavities. In a single half-century, a glacier can drive enormous segments of rock down its slopes. Unaware of human time, it thinks in centuries. But time, which is not unaware of glaciers, ends up grinding them down. Starting in July, the sea of ice becomes a dirty, pebble-lined highway in complete disarray; we struggle to imagine the walls of intense green, the emerald-coloured canyons, and the secret caves that lie beneath its surface.

Today, the cold is no longer the engineer of the Alps. The permafrost that held boulders together is melting, and rocks are falling. More than ever, snow is something that belongs to yesterday, as in the work of François Villon: it's inextricably linked with nostalgia. Where snow is concerned, we oscillate between two forms of fear: that of an all-encompassing glaciation, which obsessed people as recently as the 1970s, and that of a warming planet, which haunts us today. Where our ancestors feared the coming of a new ice age that would swallow up men and the places they inhabit, we fear a generalized heat wave that will break down the equilibrium of the seasons. In fact, the metaphor can be spun in both directions; the Middle Ages even reconciled them from time to time, as in certain Breton calvaries, which represent hell as a polar region, a zone of absolute separation between God and his creatures. In this vision, being in hell means being alone, far from the spirit's Fountain of Life and from others. The image of a burning Gehenna is an invention of the Renaissance, for which fire consuming the bodies of sinners became a more revealing image than that of frost causing them to writhe in agony. Anyone familiar with mountains or northern climates knows that frost burns like a flame, biting you until you bleed. Extreme cold and extreme heat have the same effects. Our imaginary where cold is concerned is impoverished, Bachelard said, because it's rarely conceived of in a positive way, while heat, on the contrary, is seen as an enhancing element.[3] He cites a text by Virginia Woolf that describes a harsh winter in which birds freeze in flight and fall like stones, fish become petrified in the rivers, and travellers are themselves transformed into rocks and become landmarks on the roads. He finds these images amusing but excessive. Today, cold has once more become a blessing, a counterweight to generalized warming. The fear of losing poles and ice floes almost leads us to envy the Little Ice Age (from the fourteenth to the sixteenth century), which was marked by the most appalling famines and diseases, even if it did bring about an amazing leap forward, technologically speaking, in Europe.[4] We live in fear of the desert that threatens to sterilize our green pastures (in February 2021, a sirocco from North Africa covered every mountain in the Alps with a fine ochre dust; the air became orange, and even two months later, snowdrifts still displayed, in their cross-sections, a thin yellow line, like a layer of sandy coulis inside of a pastry). It's strange to reread today the writings of poets or geologists who, barely 150 years ago, were convinced that an era of unprecedented Siberian harshness was going to ravage the earth and bring an end to civilization. Today, glaciers are retreating, and we shed tears for their inevitable disappearance. We pity and seek to save the very entities from which our ancestors fled. They're retracting in the same way as the gums of old people who have lost their teeth withdraw into their mouths. The Church saw the slopes of glaciers as representing the souls of sinners marching to atone for their transgressions. We find these superstitions almost enchanting, suffering as we do for having mastered nature all too well. Our distress is borne of a triumph, not a defeat. For some, the mountain is an adversary who must be defeated; for others, it's a resource that should be exploited; for others still, it is an 'enchanting garden', in the words of Gaston Rebuffat, that must be cultivated with tenderness, even when its enchantment turns into fury. We must cherish today what terrified us just yesterday.

CHAPTER 11

# Death in Chains?

> An astonishing happiness welled up in me, but I could not
> define it. Everything was so new, so utterly unprecedented.
> ... An enormous gulf was between me and the world. This
> was a different universe – withered, desert, lifeless; a fantastic
> universe where the presence of man was not foreseen, perhaps
> not desired. We were braving an interdict, overstepping a
> boundary, and yet we had no fear as we continued upward.
>
> MAURICE HERZOG, *ANNAPURNA: THE FIRST CONQUEST OF AN*
> *8,000-METER PEAK*[1]

It's not by accident that the mountain is lethal: this is its
very nature, and it becomes all the more deadly when men
try to subdue it or domesticate it. When this happens, even
the most beautiful ascents turn tragic, running aground
or ending with people going missing. An easy ascent gives
rise to polite applause, but the lonely figures of climbers
who died from cold or exhaustion move us. Their failure
turns them into legends while they lie buried in their frosty
shroud. Every generation produces its share of audacious
risk-takers. These people need to defy death to feel human,

but death always wins out in the end. These great paladins of high altitudes enjoy nothing more than dancing with the Grim Reaper. Someone like Lionel Terray, for example, who aimed not for useless conquests but for impossible ones. His entire life, up until his fatal fall in the Vercors, was a succession of near misses, of delayed suicides. He found his own form of freedom at the border between life and death. Speaking of his return from Annapurna in 1950 – alongside an ill and exhausted Maurice Herzog, whose surgeon kept cutting off his extremities like so many onion skins every time the train stopped (enormous worms had colonized his wounds and were devouring their necrotized flesh) – Terray wrote: 'as the dream faded, we returned to earth in a fearful mix-up of pain and joy, heroism and cowardice, grandeur and meanness'.[2] For those who took part in this mad expedition – almost all of them came close to not returning – they were terrified not so much of death as of serious injury: some lost their sight, others lost arms and legs. A diminished existence is worse than one that is abolished. The most robust among them continuously rubbed the inert hands and feet of Lachenal and Herzog, for hours on end, so as to bring the blood back into their fingers and toes. They had spent too much time in the dead zone (the region from 7,500 to 8,000 metres in which humans, lacking oxygen, begin an irreversible deterioration), and were in danger of paying a dear price for it. 'I felt immensely fragile, at the mercy of the implacable forces of fate',[3] writes Walter Bonatti about a different climb, this one in the Alps. Taking up the challenge of dangerous places means putting yourself at the disposal of the great and enigmatic lady known as death.

In its very difficulty, every mountain range makes our desire to master it appear ridiculous: we're nothing but aggressive dwarves who are keen to tame giants. The many deaths that plunge the Alps and Pyrenees into mourning each year are the proof of this: these ranges are killers who couldn't care less about the insects who tickle them as they climb; their slopes are strewn with shrines, crosses, cairns. At the Trou de la Mouche, a modest pass (2,500 metres) in the Aravis in the shape of an arc, there is a commemorative plaque that evokes – without giving any details – the recent death of a twenty-four-year-old soldier. This reminder sends chills down our spine. We'd love to know what happened to him, whether he died of cold or was struck by lightning, whether he was the victim of a dizzy spell or a bad fall. Most of the graves in the Chamonix cemetery, which are all deeply moving, are linked to accidents that took place in the Alps, whether recently or long ago. Thank God not every ascent comes down to the maniacal fury, similar to addiction, of the desire to defeat the mountain at all costs. A far better approach is that anarchy of the heights championed by Reinhold Messner, among others, which views the most formidable rock faces as a space of freedom – but within a framework of discipline and rules.[4] The old saying is true: you must want what's possible rather than doing whatever you want. And yet you're always capable of more than you believe. Young people, before they attain this practical wisdom, try to rub up against excess and give themselves superhuman tests. Every feat achieved by someone older than them is like a challenge they feel they have to match. Every passion requires a ferryman of sorts who paves the way, seeking to create his own school and gain disciples as he does so. Lionel Terray died in 1965 after a lethal fall on the Arêtes du Gerbier in the Vercors – on a 400-metre rock face that is certainly vertiginous, but far from the most difficult of the climbs he was acquainted with. As for Lachenal, he returned from Annapurna with serious injuries and took up car racing for a while before falling into a crevasse on 25 November 1955 as he was skiing the Vallée Blanche. A return to normal life was inconceivable for either of these men. The idea of ageing – in other words, settling down – after lives of such high intensity, of accepting a decrease in their vitality, was simply not something worth considering. The overused body bows out after a certain age. Lionel Terray foresaw this in his own mournful way: 'If truly no stone, no tower of ice, no crevasse lies somewhere in wait for me, the day will come when, old and tired, I find peace among the animals and flowers. The wheel will have turned full circle: I will be at last the simple peasant that once, as a child, I dreamed of becoming.'[5] For the knights of the abyss, no coming to terms with everyday life is possible.

How is it possible to survive permanent vertigo? This is the question all adventurers – all artists of the mortal challenge – ask themselves: the shame of old age is worse to them than any precipice. The desire to conquer mountain peaks reaches its limits in the decline of our physical strength around the age of forty-five or fifty. There comes a time when the risks, the sheer length of the climbs, the ability go four or five days without sleeping (or almost) and to surmount steep sections of climbs, start to take their toll on even the hardiest constitutions. There's a link between climbers and pianists: both practise the art of finding solutions for tricky passages, embracing several contradictory elements at once; the former must drag himself along without falling, while the latter must carry a melody forth without coming up short, and coordinate the efforts of both of his hands. The only difference is that the virtuoso doesn't risk his life – he only runs the risk of hitting the wrong notes. The thrill of summits that are reputed to be impregnable, of the north faces of mountains, of bivouacs in the middle of storms; the desire to become human spiders able to defy sheer rock faces and vertical walls, scraping and scratching with their fingernails to move forward – all of this is reserved for the tiny aristocracy of absolute risk. To join them, you need energy, an incomparable musculature, and a courage approaching pure madness. Freeing yourself from the forces of gravity means living on a knife edge, and opening the door to the risk of death (even if this risk is lessened by the existence of rescue squads). It's an ecstasy that borders on self-annihilation; for some, it's a state of trance that pushes them to climb at such high speeds without worrying about the risks they run. As Lionel Terray asked while on the north face of the Eiger with Louis Lachenal: 'What mad pride forced us to abandon the sweetness of life for this vertical desert?'[6]

How, then, would it be possible for these adventurers not to dream of a glorious death that would put to shame the pitiful deaths of ordinary people? The dynamics of the heights they inhabit leads the most radical of these adventurers to take themselves for gods, to consider themselves as having risen above the human condition in these cathedrals without altars. Their life on the edge makes them susceptible to what Lionel Terray calls 'the sensation of escaping from the laws of gravity, of dancing on space'.[7] They wilfully submit themselves to hardships of an unparalleled severity and cruelty. Terray writes the following of himself and Lachenal: 'Our ease and rapidity of movement had become in a sense unnatural, and we had practically evolved into a new kind of alpine animal, half way between the monkey and the mountain goat. We could run uphill for hours, climb faces as though they were step-ladders, and rush down gullies in apparent defiance of the laws of gravity.'[8] He even speaks of his ascent of the Matterhorn, that immense mineral flame, as a 'parade for the mountain goats'.[9]

Mountains are the home of simple hierarchies: low valleys and sparkling heights; ordinary men and extraordinary beings. Between these extremes, there are all sorts of inter-mediary strata – compromises between lowness and purity. But the sparkling has its price: these heights are the home of the gods, not of men. Death is never far away in these places: the surveyors of high ridges always embark upon a dance with the Grim Reaper, whom they mock without ever truly leaving him behind. It is absolute freedom that they search for in these heights, one that is unrestricted by any physical or mental limits. For them, tragedy is not so much an unfortunate occurrence as the very atmosphere they inhabit. It carries with it the possibility of disap-pearing without a trace, of sacrificing this mortal coil to a higher principle – that of sovereignty. The highest summits must be conquered because they are uninhab-itable, because they are inaccessible regions where even breathing is impossible – and as such, they are the perfect site of supreme sacrifice. This is a region of being from which you're not supposed to return, a godless trial by ordeal in which only survival can prove your greatness. To approach these peaks is to rub shoulders with the Reaper, in a deliberately provocative flirtation.

The climber who has survived a near-fatal accident comes to appear as someone who has returned from beyond death, thereby demanding respect. The writer and mountaineer Sylvain Tesson, for instance, fell while scaling the façade of a chalet in Chamonix in 2014, and was left for dead. His miraculous resurrection turned him into a different man, one who is more reasonable and cautious. There's nothing we love more than someone who has thumbed his nose at death and lived to tell the story. The sheer scale of the ordeals endured by these extraordinary beings is difficult to believe: crushed or frozen fingers, nights spent hanging from stirrups in the middle of a storm, dehydration, sunburn, hunger and thirst, sharp stones that permanently disfigure the face – this happened to Anselme

Baud, who had the right side of his face and his shoulder ripped open by a falling stone while climbing above Argentière.[10] Not one of us would survive an avalanche that buried us in snow, or a bone-breaking fall. Difficult climbs recall the words of Dante: 'abandon all hope ye who enter here'. This recalls Jon Krakauer's 1997 book *Into Thin Air: A Personal Account of the Mount Everest Disaster*, which deals with a particularly lethal expedition in 1996 in which eight people died in a single day. These funambulists of the extreme seek out confrontations with the absolute, hand-to-hand battles that have no limits. What, after all, is a hero? Someone who, having defeated death, retains an aura of indestructibility. It doesn't matter if, later on, he becomes worn out, exhausted, and disappears, for the spoils he has left to history are immortal. This experience of ultimate danger is a form of contemporary romanticism. We can marvel at these superhuman achievements, but we can also, as Jules Michelet did in the nineteenth century (though mountaineering was still in its early days then), take them as mere acrobatics that profane these 'virgin peaks of light'.[11]

Everyone in the world of mountaineering is familiar with the incredible adventure of the Englishman Joe Simpson, who broke his leg on the west face of the Siula Grande (6,344 metres) in the Peruvian Andes. His climbing companion, believing that it was impossible to save him, ended up cutting the rope that was holding them together. Simpson fell into a crevasse, but found a way out and then crawled back to the base camp; the journey took him four days. He reached camp in a state of exhaustion at the very moment when his two companions, having burned his things to 'atone for the crime', were getting ready to leave. They were staggered to see this ghost return from the realm of the dead. After two years of rehabilitation and six operations, Joe Simpson, who bore no grudge toward his former companion, returned to mountaineering, only to leave it once more after having witnessed the fall of a rope team on the north face of the Eiger, a terrifying wall 1,600 metres in height.[12] Should we dance with death to extract our tribute from it? Should we launch an assault on this stronghold that has already cost the lives of thousands of prior assailants? Must we subdue it at all costs? 'Conquer or die', screamed Terray as he confronted an ice shell – a rock as compact as concrete – while he climbed the Eiger with Lachenal. For the Englishman George Mallory, death meant not only glory, but admission into mythology: Baku Yumemakura and Jiro Taniguchi even dedicated a manga series to him, *The Summit of the Gods*,[13] which was later adapted into an animated film. For mere mortals, on the contrary, death is merely an accident. To put it very simply, the Moloch of the Alps or the Himalayas only retains its sheen by demanding that its worshippers give up their lives. He needs the blood of those reckless beings who dare to climb him. His flanks, his meadows, his moraines are strewn with human and animal corpses whose number is not diminishing with the passage of time. He kills those whom he loves in a perfect logic of passion. Climbing doesn't only mean breathing cleaner air – it also means walking in the footsteps of the dead. The indifferent giant strikes both the cautious and the inattentive without warning, especially when the conditions are bad. The survivors will always be haunted by the memory of their unlucky companions: the Englishman Edward Whymper, one of the pioneers of mountaineering, thought he saw two crosses floating in the twilight sky after three of his friends fell as they descended the Matterhorn in 1865.[14] But what truly angered Whymper was the cynicism of the local guides, who only an hour after the deadly fall were already talking about how it would bring them more clients![15]

From time to time these explorers of the heights are able to dodge fatal falls, as in the case of the young Swiss geologist Albert Heim, who, as he was descending the Säntis (2,500 metres) in 1871, slipped on a firn and miraculously lived to tell the story, the snow amassed at the foot of the wall having cushioned his fall. He would remain obsessed by this experience for his entire life, drawing lessons from it that would inspire several works on imminent death: in those few fractions of a second, he felt an absolute peacefulness and lucidity, and experienced an acceleration of his mental processes, a calm in the face of the certainty of departing the world, and a desire for reconciliation.[16] But miracles are rare, and most catastrophes are the result of something absurd, a fatal error, as in the case of the Italian climber who took a shortcut to avoid bad weather while climbing in the Entrèves in 2020, using a strap she found already placed on a wall so as to rappel down it. The strap broke and she fell to her death. Or the man on a via ferrata in Thônes who failed to attach himself properly to the safety rope, lost his balance for a moment, and fell: apparently, the last word he uttered was 'Shit!', as though it were just an annoying mishap. Not all deaths are the same: some are noble, while others are risible. People don't tend to pay homage to you when you've killed yourself by accident. Often the fatal slip happens right after you've avoided the worst danger. You think you've thwarted it, but it was just waiting for you a little further along. The very worst thing for a high-elevation tightrope walker is to slip on a staircase, fall, and kill himself stupidly. It's happened. Descending a steep staircase is the be-all and end-all of climbing.

As Malraux said, death transforms life into destiny. But certain destinies transform death into a chambermaid. As Lionel Terray said: 'What we were looking for was the enormous joy simmering in our hearts, the joy that penetrates us to our very depths when, after exploring the limits of death, we can once again embrace life to the fullest.'[17] It's the game of the final plunge. As long as you don't slip stupidly while walking on a trail, or perish from being hit by a stone launched into the void by one of your companions. Sometimes when a father escapes death through a stroke of luck, it's the son (or the daughter, or the brother, or the friend) who is carried away by a snow slide, a crevasse, a loose rock. There are terrible deaths born of a moment of carelessness, and beautiful deaths born of a clear-headed confrontation with the elements. If mountaineering didn't hang a sword over the heads of those who practise it, it wouldn't possess this absurd nobility. Being attracted to the higher realms of the terrestrial sphere, far from the philistines who trample the plains, has its price – that of transgression. This is why heroes are as tiresome as they are admirable! The mountain is beautiful and never ceases to laugh. It's also an immense cemetery that I hate. 'Passers-by, remember that what you are now, we once were; what we are now, you shall be.'

# CHAPTER 12

# Protecting the Great Stone Books

It will never cease to amaze us that the Alps, the Vosges, the Jura, the Massif central, and the Pyrenees, which for centuries were places of extreme poverty and harshness, became, in the middle of the twentieth century, playgrounds for thrill-seeking city dwellers, who enriched and changed the fortunes of villages that were previously impoverished and wretched. Winter – that horrible old man winter, enemy of the poor and the homeless – has become the season of elegance. 'A week of white snow, a year of pink cheeks', as an advertisement for Megève put it in 1930. Places that were once seen simply as sites of horrible cold and snow are now viewed as ideals of health. We have colonized these places to escape the warmth of the plains, and in doing so have turned them into tourist attractions. But this domestication of altitude is also damaging in another way: as it tames places, it also chokes them. I'm speaking of the Babel that the slopes of Val d'Isère, Méribel, Chamonix, Cortina d'Ampezzo, and Zermatt have become: people speak Turkish, Japanese, Chinese, and English in a joyful linguistic disorder. How can the mountain be saved from its popularity now that the jeans-and-sneaker set have abandoned the beach? We can understand the reticence of certain climbing federations to spruce up their mountain huts and to admit new members: they're worried that an ensuing human invasion – even one that occurs only a few times per year – would threaten the natural environment. If the 'romanticism of solitude'[1] is inherent to mountaineering, this means that it can only exist as an elitist activity. If it falls prey to mass individualism, it will contradict its very being.

We go to the mountains to escape crowds, but the crowds are now there, in their leggings and ski jackets, at the feet of the slopes and in the cable cars. Indeed, we sometimes find ourselves in the midst of an extreme carnival, an alpine supermarket the size of a small city. Let us not forget the devastation brought about by ski resorts, which have sprouted up like mushrooms since the 1970s and reveal their masses of concrete as early as March: their ski lifts deface meadows; their trails are strewn with plastic, cans, and Kleenex. There's no shortage of abandoned apartment complexes that are rusting away – we should let nature swallow them back up. There's also no shortage of coarse or corrupt mayors who issue construction permits left, right, and centre, fostering the construction of chalets and apartment blocks that are doomed to remain empty. The most beautiful slopes are gutted during the summer to build cold beds that will remain unoccupied ten months of the year. The villages of Haute-Savoie, Les Contamines, La Clusaz, La Chinaillon, Megève, Combloux, and Le Tour are dotted with cranes, backhoes, and bulldozers, preparing the way for unlikely vacationers at the very moment when snow is becoming sporadic. And we find the same suburban model at work in the resort towns of the Pyrenees. Their chairlift poles look like the ruins of a vanished civilization. And even worse: there are traffic jams at the summit of Everest, and entire processions of rope teams on Mont Blanc, les Drus, and les Grandes Jorasses, leaving piles of garbage and even corpses on mountaineers' routes. Sometimes a frozen face, fixed in a grimace of pain, emerges from the snow like a mummy. Didn't the champion climber Marion Chaygneaud-Dupuy, a former trekking guide in Tibet, become – in spite of herself – the refuse collector of Everest, carrying away tons of garbage? Instead of ice and rocks, she uncovers half-century-old deposits of rubbish! This is the new form of mountain archaeology: the exploration of detritus. The most famous mountain ranges are choking on their own success. They seem to perfectly illustrate Roberto Calasso's definition of travel: the possibility, offered to everyone, of visiting places that no longer exist. A mixture of snobbery and unawareness leads thousands of strong-willed people to climb the world's most beautiful ridges at the same time, displaying a herd instinct that boggles the mind.

If we really want to preserve our mountain ranges, we'll have to adopt a few simple rules: decongesting the mountains means limiting access to them by issuing fewer permits. To properly tend our garden, we must limit the number of gardeners – in other words, we must control the flow of visitors, at least for the most popular sites. This means closing off certain high-altitude regions. People shouldn't be allowed to go anywhere they feel like going: for beauty to last, access to it must sometimes be denied. It would be a real shame if our mountains were disfigured in the name of short-term economic or 'democratic' imperatives. The true value of the mountain is the mountain itself – its very existence is a good thing.

There are at least two ways to manage nature: preservation and conservation. The great American and Canadian parks imagined by John Muir in the nineteenth century fell under the former principle, as vast territories of wilderness were turned into sanctuaries (at an enormous cost to indigenous people, who were expelled from them). The most beautiful thing about the United States, aside from a few interesting cities, is its nature: its limitless plains, its enormous deserts, its immensely varied forests. In this country, space is synonymous with freedom, whereas in Russia, the immensity of the steppe is synonymous with imprisonment. You die of despondency on the Russian plains – as in Chekhov, and also Yesenin and his 'toska', a mixture of anguish and apathy – while in the west of the United States you conquer, bounding over the magnificent barrier of the Rockies and crossing burning deserts. In the first case, you're crushed by the infinite; in the second, you're emancipated by the frontier that you constantly push back. To which we must add an important historical nuance: the American west is the land of pioneers, trappers, gold miners, and Indians who were confined, massacred, and exterminated; Siberia is the land of imprisonment, of camps, of *zeks*, of mass murder by way of remoteness and deprivation. America turned its brutal creation into a mythology, as is illustrated by the great authors who took nature as their subject matter – James Fenimore Cooper, Jim Thompson, Ron Rash, James Crawley, Richard Brautigan, and their like. In Russia, the expanse serves to confine, producing an entire prison literature of which Dostoyevsky's *House of the Dead* remains the prototype. Russia has never left the Gulag behind.

Conservation has a different aim, that of exploiting the resources of a territory via tourism, agriculture, or breeding, but without doing any harm to it – in other words, making human activity compatible with a respect for fauna and flora. Our mountain pastures arise from this idea, and the politics of intelligent care that it promotes. The mountain is not our property – it is handed down to us as a rare good that we must respect. In the near future, access to the most popular summits will be limited, as will the ability to climb to peaks that are in danger of degrading. With all due respect to the financial gluttony of resort towns, the time of unlimited appropriation is over. Perhaps we should create the category of 'aesthetic crime' in international law: any construction that lastingly disfigures a natural site, a valley or a mountain, must be destroyed; anyone who violates a landscape should be punished. Nature does not give us the right to destroy it, but rather imposes upon us an obligation to protect it. We can imagine that certain particularly hideous resorts will be demolished, their land returned to forest or meadows. Sometimes you have to separate man from nature in order to reconcile them. It's good to maintain spaces of inhumanity and of absolute harshness on the globe, in which wildlife makes its own law.

Do we need to think like a mountain, as the American naturalist Aldo Leopold claimed at the beginning of the twentieth century? Hear the voices of snow, cliffs, streams; give a juridical status to meadows, pine forests, boulders; consider all of these as subjects under the law? But the only way for these entities to plead their case is by way of a lawyer. Who will defend the rights of a lake or a wetland, who will give voice to fauna and flora, if it is not one group of people in opposition to another? It's all well and good to give voting rights to horses or plane trees, or blades of grass, as the German sociologist Ulrich Beck proposed – we'll still be the ones counting the ballots. Whatever approach we take to the problem, we must admit that humans will always be the ones who give meaning and make laws: nature is an ethical subject only by proxy. In 2017, the High Court of Uttarakhand, a Himalayan state in the north of India, conferred juridical personhood (though the supreme court would later contest this ruling) upon the Gangotri and Yamunotri glaciers, both of which are important sites of pilgrimage for Hindus, and the first of which is the source of the sacred Ganges River. In the same way, the parliament of New Zealand, jointly with the British crown, recognized the Māori people as the lawful guardians of the sacred mountain Taranaki. These are strong gestures that, far from cancelling out the role of humans, in fact broaden their responsibility to include all natural objects, of which they now become the guardian. It's our duty to take care of the mountain just as we would take care of any fragile subject whose apparent solidity cannot withstand an invasion of well-intentioned bipeds. It's at once a matter of protecting it and of protecting ourselves from it. Everything in nature speaks, but we're the ones who provide the translation. It wouldn't displease me to one day take part in the defence of a modest peak or cliff that asked for nothing more than to persist in its being, just as I do (if on a different geological time scale). It's not the lake or the meadow that thinks – it's we who lend them our hopes, our fears, our expectations. 'Just as it dominates and crushes man thought of as an individual, the mountain is threatened by men who are united into a community.'[2] This is why the mass tourism that killed our coasts is not desirable for our mountain ranges. These great stone books[3] demand our attention, discretion, and silence. Already in 1867, Michelet called on us to 'cease to profane the Alps', to 'not carry into the mountains the grossness of the plains'.[4] It's useless to try to convert those who are resistant to mountain happiness, to speak to them of the wonders they're missing. Let's preserve high altitudes for the solemnity of pilgrimage rather than the indifference of consumerism: the former requires an austerity and a restraint that are incompatible with either stylish crowds or chatty hordes. The fact that mountains repel the lazy masses is a good thing.

# CHAPTER 13

# Sublime Chaos

Those who seek to savour the infinite are of two kinds: the first love liquid immensity, while the second love verticality. The first generally prefer oceans, while the second prefer mountain ranges. Standing on a shore and contemplating the sea right to the horizon; standing in a village and gazing at the circle of summits that surrounds you. Two experiences of excess, two types of imagination. The sea is the placenta of the origin, the depth of ocean trenches, baroque creatures, dreadful storms, villainous waves. The mountain means elegant serrations seen from the plains, the play of light over the course of the day, shadow puppets during the night, and lunar mineralization above 2,000 metres. Certain islands, such as Corsica, Réunion, and the Canaries, possess the miracle of a sea–mountain fusion, as do the French and Italian Rivieras and the Spanish Basque Country.

With rare exceptions, such as the work of Ferdinand Ramuz, Roger Frison-Roche, Erri De Luca, Michel Bernanos, Mario Rigoni Stern, and Paolo Cognetti, there are few great novels of the Alps.[1] They all tell the same story, more or less: the heroism of rock climbers, the struggle of the will against solid matter, hibernation in the high valleys. Geography dictates what the pen ends up writing, which limits the voracity of a truly overflowing imagination. Thomas Mann's *Magic Mountain* is a book about tuberculosis and sanatoriums in which the Alps are nothing more than the décor – the story is one of a confinement within a confinement. And René Daumal's *Mount Analogue* is an unfinished symbolic meditation. There's no alpine equivalent of Melville, Conrad, Stevenson, or Cendrars. The only common theme in the two universes is that of the storm, which is abominable at sea and terrifying in the mountains, pouring litres of water, stones, and hail on the daring. The ocean is more varied, as it links lands and continents and fosters dreams of adventures and discoveries; the port is the preface to the trip and is often substituted for the latter. The sea means an expanding soul in an endless void; the mountain means fullness and even surplus or excess. On the one hand, you set sail, perhaps gaining a reprieve; on the other, you gain elevation, which perhaps allows you to rise above. The proclivity for the sea is haunted by agoraphobia, the fear of immense openness; the proclivity for the mountains is haunted by claustrophobia, the fear of confined spaces. The mountaineer climbs the walls of the very prison he cherishes: it's the happiness of constantly starting over. If there were a mountain close to Paris, Stendhal wrote, it would have invigorated French literature, which would have avoided the preciousness of the seventeenth century. This is by no means certain. In France, literature is the profane form of eternal life: no other country in the world worships books and writers to the same extent. Our classics excel in the analysis of the chiaroscuro of the soul, but pay little attention to worldliness or bravery. Perhaps there's a deeper reason for their relative dryness: the decline of the culture of heroism. The climber who confronts rock faces with his ice screws and harnesses is to some degree the cousin of Don Quixote tilting against windmills. They're exceptions that we admire, but they're very difficult models to emulate. You could fill an entire library with the books that have been written for professionals of high-altitude acrobatics. These books compare the difficulties of various routes, and dispense advice for climbers of all levels. They are much more technical than literary, and fall within the domain of description far more than fiction.

We generally underestimate the wonder and the fear of the English travellers who first came upon our peaks and glaciers: this was an Atlantis in the heart of Europe, a planet contained within a planet. Our eyes have been habituated to this splendour by cinema and photography, but their eyes were open wide with amazement. These outgrowths were considered execrable by the Church and by common sentiment, and it took centuries for our gazes to consider them desirable. The mountains of Europe were never discovered – they were invented by the men of the city and of great culture, especially those Swiss humanists of the sixteenth century who presaged the enthusiasm of Romanticism.[2] Long before Rousseau, they already saw the mountains as a spectacular landscape. But mountains would only become respectable for the cultured public with the emergence, in the eighteenth century, of the notion of the sublime in the work of Immanuel Kant and Edmund Burke: the notion refers to those objects of vision that strike us by their disproportionate nature, transcend the classical idea of beauty, and give rise to a delicious terror or terrible joy within us (as long as our lives are not threatened by the experience). The spectacle of an avalanche hurtling down a slope for several kilometres transports us with its furious cannonade and its blast of air, so long as we're not harmed by it. 'The amusing thing about my taste for steep places is, that I am very fond of the feeling of giddiness which they give rise to, provided I am in a safe position.'[3] The savagery of nature has become the nourishment the soul needs to elevate itself: this cruel mother is ruthless, but her coldness moves us deeply. The notion of the sublime allows us to get beyond the opposition between the beautiful and the ugly. An amorphous landscape can be magnificent if it brings us beyond ourselves. Plato, speaking of Socrates, told us long ago that beauty puts us to sleep, but ugliness electrifies us.

A vital drama plays out at high altitudes, that of a passage between two kingdoms: triviality and intensity, profane and sacred. To climb is always to move toward the gods, even for nonbelievers. Everything that elevates ordinary life above itself is worthy of celebration. Elevation: I only exist insofar as I have been torn from my natural inertia and forced to look up. People of every age can be classified according to the energy they exert – the energy they burn and the energy they consume. Ageing well means maintaining large supplies of strength within oneself, strength that pushes us forward and that can be stored and renewed like a battery. Energy creates itself in expending itself – it dies in apathy. The real danger of old age is atony, the weariness that takes itself as philosophical. The region of great heights is a rarefied region, itself divided into several stages one must cross before arriving at the peaks where the air thins. You pass from the picturesque to the astounding, and from the astounding to the dangerous. Mountain valleys are generally sad, covered in factories, public housing, retail parks. Like so many unappealing chaperones that point the way toward the revelations of the great heights – such that climbing in a car or a bus means passing from mediocrity to an optical breathing-in of the landscape as it unfurls itself in a majestic amphitheatre. You pass from one universe to another as you rise, leaving behind you the world of baseness. And when it's time to go back down to the plains, it always feels like a punishment, a passage from bright light to shadows, from excellence to banality.

Why are mountains so beautiful? This question was the title of a lecture given by Franz Schrader, cousin of Élisée Reclus, at the *Club alpin français* in Paris in 1897.[4] His answer: 'Because in the mountains, reality takes on the hues of illusion.' An excellent response, one worthy of a landscape painter. For my part, I'd say this about the beauty of the Alps and the Pyrenees: the splendour of the first appearance you see from afar; the wonder of exploration you see up close. The sight of Mont Blanc, like a hood perched between the canines of the Drus and the fangs of the Aiguilles Vertes, and that of the Pic du Midi d'Ossau seen from Pau, are always a shock. To arrive in Savoie from Bellegarde by highway, after passing the foothills of the Jura, is to be astounded by the emergence of gleaming white giants, whose incredible diversity is astonishing. It's a beautiful surge of verticality that unites pride and sensitivity. Turrets, clock towers, donjons, minarets: the eye is unceasingly solicited and amazed. To climb via these hairpin turns is to discover the many aspects of each stage of the mountain, on each slope: hamlets, lakes, forests, waterfalls, gorges, new points of view. Mountains are not only beautiful, they're extravagant. The highlands tower over the earth like a different kind of region, one with its own laws and perspectives. The winter landscapes evoke the chimeras of our cathedrals – gargoyles or geometrical enigmas. The slopes bristle with frozen roosters' combs, fleeting monoliths, smooth and sparkling curves. Flames seem to emerge from the granite ridges that light up at certain times of the day. A peak looks like a painting by a mad artist who has at once painted a pyramid, a tetrahedron, an apse, a cyclopean landslide, hats placed upon domes, and fragments of meteorites breaking into rocks – all the while mixing up verticality and horizontality. Regrettable eccentricities that would have saddened minds from previous ages. The high mountains form an Escher-like space with multiple dimensions that have been set down haphazardly and in complete disregard for symmetry – with the exception of summits, which stand guard over all this chaos like so many fearsome sentinels. To climb is to undertake an exercise of endless celebration: being enraptured by the grace of an ibex, the shimmering of a firn, the jutting of a peak that looks like a gash in the fabric of the sky. You always see a mountain anew; its landscapes change from one hour or day to the next. Peaks appear and disappear, revolving like sets in a theatre.

To mature is to broaden the sphere of your appetites. As we climb, we learn to distinguish at least two types of beauty: a peaceful one, formed from the harmony between men and their environment, which we might find in low mountains; and a more irregular kind of beauty that lies beyond the first one, made of up of dissymmetry, jagged peaks, screes. Beauty is the reward for effort: the horizon enchants the one who witnesses it after a tough climb. Robert Macfarlane writes that until the 1700s, 'travellers who had to cross the Alpine passes often chose to be blindfolded in order to prevent them being terrified by the appearance of the peaks. When the philosopher Bishop Berkeley traversed Mont Cenis on horseback in 1714, he recorded being very much "put out of humour by the most horrible precipices."'[5] What a difference between this and Rousseau, who writes in the *Confessions* (which appeared in 1782 and 1789): 'My idea of a beautiful country is already known. No flat country, however beautiful, has ever seemed so to my eyes. I must have mountain torrents, rocks, firs, dark forests, mountains, steep roads to climb or descend, precipices at my side to frighten me.'[6] Barely a half century separates these two reflections, and yet so much has changed: with Rousseau, the shiver he feels has become an artistic ingredient. There is a pleasure in potential disaster: as all lovers of horror films know, terror is delicious when it moves us without affecting us. Taking delight in frightening or majestic spectacles is common among civilized peoples who seek to spice up their daily lives with the possibility of annihilation, and thereby to relish their own insignificance. Terrifying ice slides, the furious explosions of storms, steep passageways that put us off balance: this is what our eyes now demand to see.

Yesterday's ugliness is today's beauty – a beauty to which today, in the twenty-first century, we must add a sense of the mountain's fragility. Unlike the dead perfection of postcards, what is magnificent in the mountains is often very close to what is monstrous. Beauty thus takes possession, little by little, of that which negates it – the immense, the grotesque, the colossal – through a slow conquest of its antitheses. The mountain is never so formidable as when it disturbs our frameworks. Its monstrosity is astounding, its gracelessness beyond all categories. The delicate horror it inspires in us is analogous to the feeling of someone who has barely escaped from an avalanche and has felt the breath of death on his heels. And exquisite powerlessness is born of the chaos of the elements. An accident of geology has been turned into a poetic jewel.

# Epilogue: Once You've Reached the Summit, Keep Climbing[1]

How do you define a lover of mountains? It's anyone who trembles with pleasure at the first snowfall on the meadows, who quivers before the sun-lit belfry of a summit, whose heart skips before the minaret of a sharp peak. And who takes pleasure in the fact that Everest grows by five millimetres per year, that the mountain chains continue to rise: perhaps our descendants will always have white Christmases, so long as they're prepared to climb a bit. All the summits I'll never climb enchant me and would fill at least three more lifetimes if reincarnation existed.

Mountains continue to fascinate me, and I don't have too many years left to decipher them. Climbing, for me, remains the easiest way to escape the inevitability of time. It's a ritual of lustration. When I drag myself wearily onto a platform, when I climb an escarpment and arrive, exhausted, on a windswept crest, it's not the summit I've conquered but my own inertia: the most beautiful victory you can hope for is the victory over yourself. Overwhelmed by the incredible spectacle, I open my bag and share nuts, bread, and cheese with my companions. In the grip of emotion, I contemplate the incredible peaks and the sparkling mirrors of the purplish-blue walls of glaciers. As I descend, I don't forget to admire the blue bells of the gentians, the sprouts of arnica, the blueberries, the bluebonnets, and the clumps of rampions stuck in the cracks of rocks. Perhaps everyone has his own little portable hill that he's proud of having climbed. You have to challenge yourself with unattainable goals right to the end. Nothing is great but that which makes us greater, and what pulls us toward the sky is truly immense. The slope is always new for the one who has wandered upon it for years. There's never boredom in repeating the same thing: it's like you're doing it for the first time, even if you've done it a hundred times. I've never tamed death, but I have turned back time once or twice.

Absurdly perched upon the final levels of existence, we have no choice but to keep going, step by step. Life has often been compared to a ladder, but as we climb, we realize when we reach the final rungs that the ladder isn't leaning against any wall – it simply hangs out into the void. We become like those characters in cartoons who run off a cliff and keep making a pedalling motion with their legs. We must continue to climb as though the ascent never ended. Once you reach the summit, you must find others that challenge you, but which you couldn't see before because you were too preoccupied with the first one.

It's vital to cheat time – those figures written on your birth certificate – right to the end: nothing, and especially not the passing years, ever satisfies your thirst for existence. The mountain has taught me a fundamental lesson: the greatest misery occurs when your desires are extinguished. In altitude, like in love, it's imperative to keep pushing back your best-by date. Regardless of your age, your eyes must be bigger than your stomach: your desires must bring you beyond the realm of what is merely possible. You must balance weakening with ambition, and display a boundless appetite. So that the fervour that links us to the world never lets up.

Right up to the point at which the shade says to you: *Game over*.

But isn't the realm of shades itself a succession of peaks to climb, one more alpine barrier?

Who knows?

# Notes

*Preamble*

1 Georges Simenon, *La Mauvaise Étoile*, Folio-Gallimard, 1938, p. 87.


*1 Where Goes the White When Melts the Snow?*

1 Richard Brautigan, *Tokyo Mountain Express*, Dell, 1980, p. 13.
2 Lewis Carroll, *Through the Looking-Glass, and What Alice Found There*, SeaWolf Press, 2018, p. 4.
3 Trans.: *Sapine* sounds like *sa pine*, which means 'his prick'.
4 Arthur Rimbaud, *Complete Works, Selected Letters: A Bilingual Edition*, trans. Wallace Fowlie, revised by Seth Whidden, University of Chicago Press, 2005, p. 303.


*2 Why Climb?*

1 Reinhold Messner, *Le Sur-vivant*, Points-Seuil, 2017, p. 231. [Trans.: The German reads 'Was wollten wir hier?' See Messner, *Über Leben*, Malik Verlag, 2014, p. 198.]
2 Let me also note Patrick Dupouey's excellent book that deals with this theme: *Pourquoi grimper sur les montagnes?*, Guérin, 2012.

3 Robert Macfarlane, *Mountains of the Mind: A History of a Fascination*, Granta Books, 2003.

## 3 Our Universal Mother

1 Mahatma Gandhi, *How to Serve the Cow*, Ahmedabad, 1954. [Trans.: These passages can be found online: <https://www.mkgandhi.org/momgandhi/chap81.htm>, <https://www.mkgandhi.org/my_religion/38cow_protection.htm>, <https://www.mkgandhi.org/articles/mahatma-gandhis-views-on-cow.html>.]

## 4 The Mesmerizing Confederation

1 *The Journals of André Gide, Vol. 1: 1889–1913*, trans. Justin O'Brien, Secker & Warburg, 1948, p. 314.
2 Cited by Antoine de Baecque, *La Traversée des alpes*, Gallimard, Bibliothèque des histoires, 2014, p. 302.
3 Cited by Thierry Dufrêne, 'La montagne de verre et les enjeux artistiques du thème de cristal', in *Le Sentiment de la montagne*, Musée de Grenoble, 1998, p. 86.
4 Alphonse Daudet, *Tartarin on the Alps*, trans. Henry Frith, J. M. Dent and Co., 1896, pp. 117–18.
5 Ibid., p. 119.

## 5 The Show-Offs and the Yokels

1 Authored by Christophe, it was published from 1889 to 1893 by the publisher Armand Colin.
2 Trans.: *Les Bidochon* is a French comic created by the writer and artist Binet. The comic is a satirical portrayal of the fictitious Bidochon family, who are presented as the 'average' French family. The name has come to be used in a slightly insulting way, somewhat akin to the term 'bumpkin' in English.

3 Quoted in Gaston Bachelard, *La Terre et les rêveries de la volonté*, Corti, 1947, p. 348.
4 See de Baecque, *La Traversée des alpes*, pp. 63–6.
5 Philippe Claudel, *Le Lieu essentiel. Entretiens avec Fabrice Lardreau*, Arthaud, 2018.
6 Lionel Terray, *Conquistadors of the Useless: From the Alps to Annapurna*, trans. Geoffrey Sutton, Gollancz, 1963, p. 229.
7 Walter Bonatti, *The Mountains of My Life*, trans. Robert Marshall, Modern Library, 2001, p. 279.
8 Félicité Herzog, *Un Héros*, Grasset, 2012.

## 6 Lived Experiences

1 Frédéric Gros, *A Philosophy of Walking*, trans. John Howe, Verso, 2014, p. 97.
2 Stéphanie Bodet, *À la Verticale de soi*, Guérin, 2016, pp. 77–8.
3 Friedrich Nietzsche, *Selected Letters of Friedrich Nietzsche*, trans. Anthony M. Ludovici, Doubleday, 1921, p. 169.
4 Friedrich Nietzsche, *Human, All Too Human II and Unpublished Fragments from the Period of Human, All Too Human II (Spring 1878–Fall 1879)*, trans. Gary Handwerk, Stanford University Press, 2013, §295, p. 278.
5 Friedrich Nietzsche, *Ecce Homo: How to Become What You Are*, trans. Duncan Large, Oxford University Press, 2007, §3, p. 4.
6 Friedrich Nietzsche, *The Gay Science*, trans. Josefine Nauckhoff, Cambridge University Press, 2001, §283, p. 161.
7 Joe Simpson, *The Beckoning Silence*, The Mountaineers Books, 2003, pp. 107–8.
8 Friedrich Nietzsche, *Thus Spoke Zarathustra: A Book for All and None*, trans. Adrian Del Caro, Cambridge University Press, 2006, 'On Passing By', p. 141.
9 Ibid., 'On the Rabble', p. 76.
10 Gaston Bachelard, *L'Air et les songes*, Biblios essais, 2020, pp. 206–7.

11 Nietzsche, *Thus Spoke Zarathustra*, §5, p. 10.
12 On the Abalakov brothers, see the excellent *Alpinistes de Staline* by Cédric Gras (Stock, 2020), which won the Albert Londres Prize.

## 7 The Aesthetics of the Adventurer

1 Quoted in Simpson, *The Beckoning Silence*, p. 70.
2 Henry David Thoreau, *Walking*, Riverside Press, 1914, p. 6.
3 Trans.: Bruckner here plays on the words *penser*, to think, and *panser*, to bandage, which have the same pronunciation.
4 Nancy Huston, *Marcher avec les philosophes*, Philo Mag Éditeurs, 2018, p. 101.
5 In *Le Sur-vivant*, Reinhold Messner cites, among the stylists of 'clean climbing', the American Royal Robbins and the Slovene Marko Prezelj (p. 302).

## 8 The Two Faces of the Abyss

1 Macfarlane, *Mountains of the Mind*, p. 99.
2 Ibid., pp. 91–2.
3 Ibid., p. 71.
4 Lionel Daudet, *Le Tour de la France, exactement*, Stock, 2014.
5 In *Ceux qui vont en montagne* (PUG, 2020), Bernard Amy speaks of the nostalgia of seniors who are caught in a frenzy of counting: 'Their list of challenges gets longer and longer. At the end of the winter, they explain that they've gone skiing forty times for a total elevation gain of 10,000 metres. In the spring, they speak to you condescendingly, amazed that "unlike them, you still haven't done any sixth-degree or even (on good days) seventh-degree climbs"' (pp. 61–2). [Trans.: These numbers refer to numerical grades whereby climbs in France are rated according to difficulty.]
6 Terray, *Conquistadors of the Useless*, p. 152.
7 Ibid., p. 153.

## 9 Reynard and Isengrim

1 Michel Pastoureau, *Le Loup, une histoire culturelle*, Seuil, 2019, p. 13.
2 Ibid., p. 105.
3 Jack London, *The Call of the Wild*, Macmillan, 1919, pp. 27–8.
4 Ibid., p. 44.
5 Jack London, *White Fang*, Macmillan, 1911, p. 26.
6 Cited by de Baecque in *La Traversée des alpes*, pp. 313–14.
7 See de Baecque, *La Traversée des alpes*, p. 350.
8 See Nastassja Martin, *In the Eye of the Wild*, trans. Sophie R. Lewis, New York Review Books, 2021.
9 London, *White Fang*, p. 107.
10 Pablo Servigne, Raphaël Stephens, and Gauthier Chapelle, *Another End of the World Is Possible: Living the Collapse (and not merely surviving it)*, trans. Geoffrey Samuel, Polity, 2021, p. 180.
11 Jean-Marc Rochette, *Le Loup*, Casterman, 2019, with a postscript by Baptiste Morizot.
12 See Geoffroy Delorme, *Deer Man: Seven Years of Living in the Wild*, trans. Shaun Whiteside, Greystone Books, 2022.
13 An example is the philosopher and wolf-tracker Baptiste Morizot, *Sur la piste animale*, Actes Sud, 2017.
14 Bonatti, *The Mountains of My Life*, p. 118.

## 10 Loving What Terrifies Us

1 Immanuel Kant, *Critique of Judgment*, trans. Werner S. Pluhar, Hackett, 1987, §25, p. 105.
2 Cited in Macfarlane, *Mountains of the Mind*, p. 222.
3 Gaston Bachelard, *La Terre et les rêveries de la volonté*, Les Massicotés, pp. 216–17.
4 This is one of the many themes Robert Macfarlane deals with in his brilliant *Mountains of the Mind*.

## 11 Death in Chains?

1 Maurice Herzog, *Annapurna: The First Conquest of an 8,000-Meter Peak*, trans. Nea Morin and Janet Adam Smith, Lyons Press, 2010, p. 143.
2 Terray, *Conquistadors of the Useless*, p. 295.
3 Bonatti, *The Mountains of My Life*, p. 256.
4 Messner, *Le Sur-vivant*, p. 362.
5 Terray, *Conquistadors of the Useless*, p. 347.
6 Ibid., p. 201.
7 Ibid., p. 198.
8 Ibid., p. 132.
9 Ibid., p. 134.
10 Anselme Baud, *Au pays des terres hautes*, Kero, 2018, p. 125.
11 Jules Michelet, *The Mountain*, trans. W. H. D. Adams, T. Nelson and Sons, 1872, p. 77.
12 See Joe Simpson, *Touching the Void: The True Story of One Man's Survival*, Harper Perennial, 1998; Simpson, *The Beckoning Silence*.
13 Baku Yumemakura and Jiro Taniguchi, *The Summit of the Gods*, trans. Kumar Sivasubramanian, Ponent Mon, 2009–2015 (for vols 1–5).
14 Macfarlane, *Mountains of the Mind*, p. 216. Whymper recounts this tragedy in *Scrambles Amongst the Alps in the Years 1860–69*, John Murray, 1900, pp. 387–8.
15 Whymper, *Scrambles Amongst the Alps*, p. 389.
16 See Thomas Vennin, *Les Hallucinés. Un voyage dans les délires d'altitude*, Paulsen, 2020, pp. 85–7.
17 Quoted in Paul Yonnet, *La Montagne et la mort*, Éditions de Fallois, 2003, p. 55.

## 12 Protecting the Great Stone Books

1 See Anne-Laure Boch's excellent book *L'Euphorie des cimes*, Transboréal, 2017, pp. 30–1.

2 Ibid., p. 32.
3 Trans.: 'The great stone book' is a geological term that arose in the 1800s, conveying the idea that 'the mountains provided a venue where it was possible to browse the archives of the earth' (Macfarlane, *Mountains of the Mind*, p. 49).
4 Michelet, *The Mountain*, p. 291.

## 13 Sublime Chaos

1 As Belinda Cannone remarks in *La Forme du monde*, Versant intime, 2019, pp. 55–6.
2 See Philippe Joutard, 'Redécouverte de la montagne au XVIII$^e$ siècle, création d'une mode', in *Le Sentiment de la montagne*, p. 11.
3 Jean-Jacques Rousseau, *Confessions*, ed. P. N. Furbank, Knopf, 1992, p. 157 (Book IV).
4 Franz Schrader, *À quoi tient la beauté des montagnes?*, Isolato, 2010. Lecture de Joël Cornuault.
5 Macfarlane, *Mountains of the Mind*, pp. 145–6.
6 Rousseau, *Confessions*, pp. 156–7 (Book IV).

## Epilogue

1 Tibetan proverb.